Finding God in the Psalms

Finding God in the Psalms

Sing, pray, live

TOM WRIGHT

Originally published in the United States of America in 2013
as *The Case for the Psalms: Why they are essential*
by HarperCollins Publishers, New York

First published in Great Britain in 2014

Society for Promoting Christian Knowledge
36 Causton Street
London SW1P 4ST
www.spckpublishing.co.uk

British Library Cataloguing-in-Publication Data
A catalogue record for this book is available from the British Library

ISBN 978–0–281–06989–7
eBook ISBN 978–0–281–06993–4

First printed in Great Britain by Ashford Colour Press
Subsequently digitally printed in Great Britain

eBook by Graphicraft Limited, Hong Kong

Produced on paper from sustainable forests

For Annabel

I shall walk at liberty, for I have sought your precepts.
Psalm 119.45

Contents

Chapter 1

Introduction

THIS BOOK IS A PERSONAL PLEA. THE PSALMS, which make up the great hymnbook at the heart of the Bible, have been the daily lifeblood of Christians, and of course the Jewish people, from the earliest times. Yet in many Christian circles today, the Psalms are simply not used. And in many places where they are still used, whether said or sung, they are often reduced to a few verses to be recited as a 'filler' between other parts of the liturgy or worship services. In the latter case, people often don't seem to realize what they're singing. In the former case, they don't seem to realize what they're missing. This book is an attempt to reverse those trends. I see this as an urgent task.

Suppose the Psalms had been lost and had never been printed in any Bibles or prayer books. Suppose they then turned up in a faded but still legible scroll, discovered by archaeologists in the sands of Jordan or Egypt. What would happen? When deciphered and translated, they would be on the front page of every newspaper in the world. Many scholars from many disciplines would marvel at the beauty and content of these ancient worship songs and poems.

The Psalms are among the oldest poems in the world, and they still rank with any poetry in any culture, ancient or modern, from anywhere in the world. They are full of power and passion, horrendous misery and unrestrained jubilation, tender sensitivity and powerful hope. Anyone at all whose heart is open to new dimensions of human experience, anyone who loves good writing, anyone who wants a window into the bright lights and dark corners of the human soul – anyone open to the beautiful expression of a larger vision of reality should react to these poems like someone who hasn't had a good meal for a week or two. It's all here.

And astonishingly, it doesn't get lost in translation. Most poetry suffers when translated into other languages because it relies for its effect on the sound and rhythm of the original words. It's true that the Hebrew of these poems is beautiful in itself for those who can experience it. But the Psalms rely for their effect on the way they set out the main themes. They say something from one angle and then repeat it from a slightly different one:

> *By the word of* YHWH *the heavens were*
> *made,*
> *and all their host by the breath of his*
> *mouth. (33.6)*

> *I will open my mouth in a parable;*
> *I will utter dark sayings from of old.*
> *(78.2)*

> *You search out my path and my lying down,*
> *and are acquainted with all my ways.*
> *(139.3)*

Even when this doesn't happen line by line, it often happens between different sections of a psalm or in the balance of the collection, or a part of it, as a whole.

The important point here is that some of the most important things we want to say remain just a little beyond even our best words. The first sentence is a

signpost to the deep reality; the second, a signpost
from a slightly different place. The reader is invited
to follow both and to see the larger, unspoken truth
looming up behind. This means that not only can the
effect be maintained in translation, but the effect is
itself one of the deepest things the Psalms are doing,
making it clear that the best human words point
beyond themselves to realities that transcend even
high poetic description. (Something similar is achieved
elsewhere in the Bible – for instance, in the provision
in Genesis of *two* creation stories, offering two picture-
language images for a reality that lies beyond either.)

All this, as I said, should capture the attention
and generate the excitement of anyone sensitive to
powerful writing on the great themes of human
life. But for those who, in whatever way, stand in
the spiritual traditions of Judaism and Christianity,
there is all that and much, much more. That makes it
all the more frustrating that the Psalms are so often
neglected today or used at best in a perfunctory and
shallow way.

In some parts of contemporary Christianity, the
Psalms are no longer used in daily and weekly worship. This is so especially at points where there has
been remarkable growth in numbers and energy, not

least through the charismatic movements in various denominations. The enormously popular 'worship songs', some of which use phrases from the Psalms here and there but most of which do not, have largely displaced, for thousands of regular and enthusiastic worshippers, the steady rhythm and deep soul-searching of the Psalms themselves. This, I believe, is a great impoverishment.

By all means write new songs. Each generation must do that. But to neglect the church's original hymnbook is, to put it bluntly, crazy. There are many ways of singing and praying the Psalms; there are styles to suit all tastes. That, indeed, is part of their enduring charm. I hope that one of the effects of this little book will be to stimulate and encourage those who lead worship in many different settings to think and pray about how to reintegrate the church's ancient prayer book into the regular and ordinary life of their fellowships. The Psalms represent the Bible's own spiritual root system for the great tree we call Christianity. You don't have to be a horticultural genius to know what will happen to the fruit on the tree if the roots are not in good condition.

But I'm not writing simply to say, 'These are important songs that we should use and try to understand.' That is true, but it puts the emphasis the wrong way round – as though the Psalms are the problem, and we should try to fit them into our world. Actually, again and again it is we, muddled and puzzled and half-believing, who are the problem; and the question is more how *we* can find our way into *their* world, into the faith and hope that shine out in one psalm after another.

As with all thoughtful Christian worship, there is a humility about this approach. Good liturgy, whether formal or informal, ought never to be simply a corporate upsurge of emotion, however 'Christian', but a fresh and awed attempt to inhabit the great unceasing liturgy that is going on all the time in the heavenly realms. (That's what those great chapters, Revelation 4 and 5, are all about.) The Psalms offer us a way of joining in a chorus of praise and prayer that has been going on for millennia and across all cultures. Not to try to inhabit them, while continuing to invent non-psalmic 'worship' based on our own feelings of the moment, risks being like a spoilt child who, taken to the summit of Table Mountain with the city and the ocean spread out before him, refuses to gaze at the view because he is playing with his Game Boy.

In particular, I propose in this book that the regular praying and singing of the Psalms is *transformative*.

It changes the way we understand some of the deepest elements of who we are, or rather, who, where, when and what we are: we are creatures of space, time and matter, and though we take our normal understandings of these for granted, it is my suggestion that the Psalms will gently but firmly transform our understandings of all of them. They do this in order that we may be changed, transformed, so that we look at the world, one another and ourselves in a radically different way, which we believe to be God's way. I hope my exposition of these themes will help to explain and communicate my own enthusiasm for the Psalms, but I hope even more that they will encourage those churches that have lost touch with the Psalms to go back to them as soon as possible, and those that use them but with little grasp of what they're about to get inside them in a new way.

The Psalms thus transform what I have called our 'worldview'. I use this term in a specific way that I have developed over the last twenty years. A 'worldview' in this sense is like a pair of spectacles: it is what you look *through*, not what you look *at*. Worldviews, in this sense, are complex and consist of the swirling combination of stories, symbols, habitual praxis and assumed answers to key questions (Who are we? Where are we? What's wrong? What's the solution? What time is it?). This developed notion of 'worldview' has its roots in some aspects of continental philosophy, though I have developed it slightly differently; I have set it all out in various places, such as the volumes in my series Christian Origins and the Question of God. There is, however, a quite different meaning of 'worldview' that has recently become popular in some circles in America, particularly under the influence of Francis Schaeffer and his disciples. There it is used to refer to a basic kit of would-be Christian assumptions that for some reason have taken on a particular political slant. That is not what I am talking about, as will become clear.

This book makes no attempt to discuss who wrote the Psalms or when. Nor do I discuss the theories as to how they have been shaped and edited into their present format. Those are important questions but not for this book. Jewish and Christian traditions see King David, a thousand years before Jesus, as the writer of the Psalms; scholarly tradition, eager as always not to appear naive or to be taken in by previous beliefs, has dated them much later – within the last three or four hundred years before Christ. Our knowledge of Israel's early history is patchy at best, forming a very uneven surface on which to hit the billiard balls of ancient evidence around the table. One cannot prove that any of the psalms go back to King David himself, but one cannot prove, either, that none of them do. Many of them clearly reflect both the language and the setting of much later periods. As with our modern hymnbooks, this may be due to subsequent editorial activity, or it may be that they were composed by writers who thought of themselves as standing within a poetic tradition they themselves believed to go back to Israel's early monarchy. These debates have sometimes reflected modern theories of 'inspiration' (does it happen through one individual or through a community?), but there is no sign that the ancient Israelites or second-Temple Jews were worried about such things.

It seems wisest to think of the Psalms, in their present form, being collected and shaped in the time of the exile in Babylon (beginning in the sixth century BC), when paradoxically the people who found it unthinkable to sing the Lord's song in a strange land may have found that actually singing those songs (and writing some new ones) was one of the few things that kept them sane and gave them hope. That they formed the basic hymnbook of the second Temple in

Jerusalem (beginning with the reconstruction of the Temple after the return from exile, which began near the transition from the sixth to the fifth century BC), as well as of the thousands of local Jewish gatherings (in 'synagogues') around the world and in the holy land itself, we should have no doubt.

A caveat is in order at this point. It is likely that in the first Temple in Jerusalem, and perhaps in the second as well, rebuilt after the exile, the actual singers were Levites who were trained to make music on behalf of all the people. As with the sacrificial cult, the people would come to the Temple, but the regular officials would perform the final act on their behalf. This doesn't mean that the majority of worshippers were ignorant of what was being sung or unmoved by the words or the music. It just means that they almost certainly had more of a sense of corporate solidarity than is common today in modern Western individualism. The worship was that of the whole people of God, even if some people were set apart, trained and equipped to offer it publicly. Away from the Temple in Jerusalem, the Jews developed centres of meeting and worship referred to as 'synagogues'. Frustratingly, we do not know as much as we would like to about how first-century Jews ordered their regular worship in the synagogues, either in the holy land itself or around the Jewish diaspora. It is highly likely, though, that the Psalms featured prominently and that ordinary worshippers were encouraged to join in and make them their own.

This means, of course, that the Psalms were the hymnbook that Jesus and his first followers would have known by heart. Even in today's world, where electronic gadgets have radically reduced the need for memorization, most of us can remember the songs, whether sacred or secular, that were popular in our childhood and teenage years. Jesus and his contemporaries would have known the Psalms inside out. Paul would have prayed and sung them from his earliest years. What Jesus believed and understood about his own identity and vocation, and what Paul came to believe and understand about Jesus's unique achievement, they believed and understood within a psalm-shaped world. That same shaping, remarkably, is open to us today. That is the burden of my song.

Because this book is more than simply an intellectual argument, I also want to draw on my own experience as an example of how the Psalms can work in the actual day-to-day business of living. So I have included an afterword entitled 'My Life with the Psalms' where, I hope, I can say by example what I have argued for in the previous chapters.

A TECHNICAL NOTE: I follow the numbering for the Psalms that is found in the Hebrew Bible, followed by almost all English versions. The exceptions are those Roman Catholic translations that follow the Latin Vulgate, which in turn was based on the Septuagint. The Septuagint (the Greek translation of scripture made by Jewish scholars in Egypt roughly two hundred years before Jesus and then used and perhaps re-edited by early Christian scribes) follows a different system, treating the Hebrew Psalms 9 and 10 as a single psalm and numbering everything after that one less than the Hebrew and English (so that, for instance, the famous 'shepherd' psalm that most English readers think of as Psalm 23 is Psalm 22). Psalms 114 and 115 are likewise combined (as 113), but 116 is divided (as 114 and 115), so that what in the Hebrew and most English versions is 117 is 116. Finally, 147 is divided (into 146 and 147), so that the last three psalms, 148, 149, and 150, join the first eight in having the same numbering in all versions. Thus in Roman Catholic Bibles and liturgies the numbering of most of the Psalms is slightly different from that in the versions based on the Hebrew.

Chapter 2

Pray and Live

I HAVE SAID IN THE INTRODUCTION WHAT I hope to achieve in this book. Underneath this hope there are two other motivations that I ought to set out as we launch into the main material. The first is personal and easily stated. The second is fuller and a bit more complicated.

First, for me to think about the Psalms is like thinking about breathing. I breathe all the time but seldom stop to think about it or about what might happen if I tried to stop. In the same way, I have sung, said and read the Psalms all of my life, from early churchgoing days in the Anglican tradition through glorious years in the English cathedral tradition, and with my own daily reading of them as a constant backdrop – or should I say backbone – for everything else. So in these reflections I am seizing an opportunity to step back and examine something that has been there throughout my life and ask, 'What are these poems that I have been praying and singing all this time? What have they been doing to me, or in me, or helping me to do or to become?' I hope that as I try to answer these questions, my readers will be encouraged and stimulated to ask the same questions for themselves.

Second, alongside that lifelong habit, I have been pondering the Psalms for a long time from the perspective of devout Jews in the second-Temple period. That is part of the regular task of anyone trying, as I have done for many years, to understand the origin of Christianity in its historical context.

The Psalms are enormously important in the New Testament, as a glance at any list of biblical quotations and allusions in the New Testament will reveal. Jesus himself quoted and referred to the Psalms in the manner of someone who had been accustomed to praying and pondering them from his earliest days. Paul referred to several psalms and wove them in quite a sophisticated way into his remarkable theology. But behind those explicit references there stands, I believe, an entire world in which Jewish people were singing and praying the Psalms day by day and month by month, allowing them to mould their character, to shape their worldview, to frame their reading of the rest of scripture, and (not least) to fuel and resource the active lives they were leading and the burning hopes that kept them trusting their God, the world's creator, even when everything seemed bleak and barren. For whichever bit of the Old Testament we take, in fact, it is always worth asking, 'How would devout Jews in the late first century BC have heard, read, sung and prayed this?' This is particularly true of the Psalms. We cannot be quite sure which Jews studied which scriptures in what way, but we are on safe ground in saying that they used the Psalms as their basic prayer book. That was the world in which Jesus grew up.

Everything we know about Jesus inclines us to say, of course, that he read the whole of Israel's scriptures, the Psalms included, in a fresh way. This was part of his own dramatically different understanding of what Israel's God was wanting to accomplish in and through his people. But his fresh vision of Israel's vocation, the sense of his own calling within that, and the sense of how Israel's scriptures pointed him in that direction and sustained him in his resolute announcement of God's kingdom, even though it led him to the cross, were nevertheless a new twist *within* that great tradition, not a move outside it.

This means that Jesus and his first followers were living within an implied worldview that they shared with their Jewish contemporaries but emphatically not with the modern Western world. As I said, 'worldview' is sometimes a tricky term. But it is still useful if we are to dig down beneath the surface of what the early Christians believed and hoped, and how they lived, and to understand, so to speak, what made them tick.

At this point it is important to prevent a regular misunderstanding. People have often supposed that the main difference between the worldview held by the early Christians and the worldview most of us grew up with is that the first is 'ancient' and the second is 'modern'. It is then often assumed that because we 'live in the modern world' we are bound to dismiss the 'ancient' worldview as out of date, prescientific, and based on ignorance and superstition and accept the 'modern' one as, supposedly, up to date and based on science, technology, and all the wisdom of a modern 'free' society. This, however, is radically misleading.

The main difference between the worldview of the first Christians and the worldview of most modern Western persons has nothing to do with 'ancient' and 'modern'. It has almost nothing to do, except at a tangent, with the development of modern science. The main difference is that the first Christians, being first-century Jews who believed that Israel's God had fulfilled his ancient promises in Jesus of Nazareth, were what I and others call 'creational monotheists': that is, they believed that the one creator God, having made the world, remained in active and dynamic relation with it. What's more, they believed that this God had promised to return to his people at the end of their long, sad years of desolation and misery to dwell in their midst and to set up his sovereign rule on earth as in heaven. And they believed that in Jesus of Nazareth, and in the power of his Spirit at work in their lives, this God had done exactly that.

The ancient Jews who shaped this belief in creational monotheism, and the early Christians who developed it in this startling new way, were doing so in a world of many philosophies and worldviews. One of these, every bit as 'ancient' as that of the first-century Jews, was the philosophy known after the name of its founder, Epicurus. The philosophy

of Epicurus, particularly in its developed exposition
by the great Roman poet Lucretius (who lived about
a century before Jesus), proposed that the world
was not created by a god or the gods and that, if
such beings existed, they were remote from the
world of humans. Our world and our own lives were
simply part of a continuing self-developing cosmos
in which change, development, decay and death itself
operated entirely under their own steam.

At a stroke, this philosophy offered liberation
from any fear of the gods or of what terrors might
be in store for people after their deaths. But by the
same stroke, it cut off any long-term or ultimate
hope. At a popular level, the message was this: shrug
your shoulders and enjoy life as best you can. Sounds
familiar? *This is the philosophy that our modern Western world has largely adopted as the norm.*

The problem we face when we read, pray or sing
parts of the Bible is not that it is 'old' and our current
philosophy is 'new' (and therefore somehow better).
The problem is that, out of many ancient worldviews,
the Bible resolutely inhabits one, and much of the
modern Western world has resolutely inhabited a different one. Our prevailing modern Western worldview is no more 'modern' than the worldview of the

first Christians. All that has happened is that many leading scientists in the eighteenth and nineteenth centuries, who were attracted to Epicureanism for quite other reasons (not least social, cultural and political), have interpreted their perfectly proper scientific observations (for instance, concerning the origin and development of different species of plants and animals) within an Epicurean framework. It has then been assumed that 'science' actually *supports* this view of a detached 'god' and a world simply doing its own thing. But this is profoundly mistaken.

Epicureanism, then, is of course an ancient worldview, but it has been retrieved in Western modernity as though it were a new thing. Creational and covenantal monotheism is likewise both ancient and modern, rooted in God's covenant with Abraham as described in the book of Genesis, elaborated in the great covenantal writings of the first five books of the Bible, developed in the traditions we find throughout the Old Testament, and still thriving where the followers of Jesus learn to pray and live his Psalm-soaked gospel. Part of my reflection in this book is that when the Psalms do their work in us and through us, they should equip us the better to live by and promote that alternative worldview. The biblical worldview,

I will suggest, is both far more ancient than Epicureanism and also far more up to date.

In order to describe the worldview the Psalms invite
us to inhabit, I have decided, as a kind of thought
experiment, to order the material in three sections.
The Psalms invite their singers, as they always have,
to live at the crossroads of *time*, *space* and *matter*.
This book explores what happens at this crossing
point – or rather, these crossing points. I don't just
mean that time, space and matter are themselves
like three roads that meet together at a certain place.
It sometimes helps to think of our own experience
in that way, as we struggle to live in the present
rather than the past or the future: Who am I, what
am I doing *now* (time), *here* (space), and in *this* body
(matter) that God has given me? That is no doubt
important. But the crossing points I have in mind are
a bit more complicated.

   I am thinking, first, of the crossroads between one
sort of time and another: our time, if you like, and
God's time, in which aspects of what we think of
as the 'past' and what we think of as the 'future'
can actually come together in what we perceive and
experience as the 'present'. I am thinking, second,

of the crossroads between one *sort* of 'place' and another: our place or space, if you like, and God's space. (In the Bible, these are often referred to as 'earth' and 'heaven', though that can be misleading because many people today assume that if 'heaven' exists, it is a long way away and a different sort of reality altogether, which isn't how the Bible sees it at all.) I am thinking, third, of the crossroads between the created order, the material world as we normally perceive it, and the way in which that creation, already 'charged with the grandeur of God', is promised that it will at the last be filled afresh, filled to overflowing, with that same grandeur or glory.

Time, space and *matter:* I have written recently about these in relation to Jesus himself (see *Simply Jesus*). I was actually rather surprised to find myself doing so, but I discovered that it was the only way to explain how some things within the four Gospels – things that seem very peculiar to us today – would have appeared quite differently to Jesus himself and his first followers. I want, in this book, to use this threefold division as a tool with which to probe more deeply into the Psalms, to explore some of the depths of these profound poems and songs that Jesus himself made his own in a new and rich way.

The Psalms, I want to suggest here, are songs and poems that help us not just to *understand* this most ancient and relevant worldview but actually to *inhabit* and *celebrate* it – this worldview in which, contrary to most modern assumptions, God's time and ours overlap and intersect, God's space and ours overlap and interlock, and even (this is the really startling one, of course) the sheer material world of God's creation is infused, suffused and flooded with God's own life and love and glory. The Psalms will indeed help us to understand all of this. But it will be an understanding that grows out of a deeper and richer kind of knowing – something that brings together imagination, insight, and love.

As you sing the Psalms, pray the Psalms and ponder the Psalms, you will find yourself drawn into a world in which certain things make sense that would not otherwise do so. In particular, you will be drawn into a world where God and Jesus make sense in a way they would not otherwise do.

That is why this book is not so much an invitation to *study* the Psalms – though that, too, is an immensely worthwhile exercise – but to *pray and live* the Psalms.

Many Christian traditions, including my own, have assumed that this is an absolutely basic component of Christian living. As I said earlier, however, some in recent years have seemed to give them up or to marginalize them, turning one or two of them into modern 'praise songs' and letting the rest lie fallow. That is the Christian equivalent of a musician who assumes she can still perform at concert level without the daily discipline of practice, or the soccer player who still expects to score goals in games without ever showing up for training. The Psalms are the steady, sustained subcurrent of healthy Christian living. They shaped the praying and vocation even of Jesus himself. They can and will do the same for us.

The Psalms do this, to begin with, simply because they are poetry set to music: a classic double art form. To write or read a poem is already to enter into a different kind of thought world from our normal patterns. A poem is not merely ordinary thought with a few turns and twiddles added on to make it pretty or memorable. A poem (a good poem, at least) uses its poetic form to probe more deeply into human experience than ordinary speech or writing is usually able to do, to pull back a veil and allow the hearer or reader to sense other dimensions. Sometimes this provokes a shock of recognition: *Yes*, we think, *I have felt exactly like that, but I'd never seen it so clearly.* Sometimes the shock is of something new: *I'd never seen that angle before, but now that I've seen it, I won't forget it.* Sometimes it's a combination of both of these, and often more besides.

But when you take a poem and set it to music, you add a further dimension still. Music is classic right-brain activity. It creates a new and wider world within which the rational analysis of the left brain can do its proper, though subordinate, work. Music already employs melody, harmony and rhythm, just as poetry employs metre, rhyme and some kind of narrative flow, or at least the unfolding of a thought or insight. But when we listen to music and when we hear or read a poem, the music or poetry fails if we sit there thinking about melody, harmony, rhythm, metre, rhyme or plotline. The point of both is to open new worlds, to take us (as we sometimes say) into a different space. I recently attended a poetry reading that didn't go on for much more than an hour, but when it was over, I felt as though I'd been on holiday for a week. I have been to concerts like that, too.

All this is true of what we might think of as 'secular' music and poetry. Think, for example, of some of the great operas or of the remarkable songs of Franz Schubert or, indeed, of Bob Dylan or Bruce Cockburn. But when the poetry in question is a set of remarkably diverse and yet remarkably coherent songs whose aim is to praise the God of Israel, to celebrate his love and power even in the midst of pain and sorrow, and indeed to bring all of human life into his presence, then there is a third dimension.

Words, music and *worship:* the words and music themselves are simultaneously *acts of* worship (all human art and skill can be and should be brought before the creator God in glad offering) and *expressions of* worship itself.

I wish this book could sing so I could make what I mean even clearer. I am, however, very much aware that there are many different styles and subcultures within the musical world and that the way I was brought up to sing the Psalms is quite different from many other ways. But I hope the point is made. The Psalms are there for every church to use in public worship, in creative and imaginative ways but also in ways that become familiar and traditional in the best sense, so that the worshippers can slip into them as one would into a comfortable suit of clothes.

They are also there for every Christian – child, woman, and man – to use in their private prayers, both in the regular discipline of morning and evening worship and in the thousand moments during the day when something happens to which the first response should be prayer, whether in praise or in panic.

The first use, of course, sustains the second. Those who pray the Psalms day by day (my tradition suggests getting through them once a month, but there are many other ways as well; I will say more about that later) are putting themselves in the position where, when faced with a sudden crisis, they will discover close at hand a line or two of a psalm that is already etched into the heart and mind and says just what they want to say, only most likely better than they could say it themselves in the heat of the moment.

This book, then, is an unashamed encouragement for all Christians to weave the Psalms into the very heart of their devotional life and to expect to find as they do this that the way they look out at the world will change bit by bit.

In part, this will happen simply because people who pray the Psalms will be worshipping the God who made them, and one of the basic spiritual laws is that you become like what you worship. More particularly, however, it will happen because people who pray the Psalms will be learning (whether they necessarily think it out like this or not) to live in God's time as well as in their own, in God's space as well as in their own, and even in and as God's 'matter' – the stuff of which we're made – as well as in and as our own. The three main sections of this book, which will follow in a moment, will set out each of these in turn. Let me say just one further word about each of them.

First, 'time'. All music and all poetry regularly have the capacity to transcend ordinary time. They call to the depths of memory and imagination, bringing the past forward into the present (memory) and envisaging the future as well (imagination).

Second, 'space'. The designers of Gothic cathedrals built them as great vaulted spaces, soaring high above ordinary human capacities. They knew perfectly well that these huge echoing arches made no sense as human habitations; unlike ordinary houses or shops, they were not built, as it were, 'to our scale'. That is because they were designed to evoke the mysterious

heavens, which are normally inaccessible to us –
except precisely when we make music. When we
sing, the sound made even by small-scale earthbound
creatures such as us rings around the rafters that we
cannot otherwise reach.

Third, 'matter'. All singers discover that to use
the human body as a musical instrument is physically, emotionally, and mentally transformative in a
way nothing else quite is. What's more, people who
learn the serious business of prayer often discover
something that therapists in other traditions sometimes stumble upon as well: that prayer encourages
a rhythm of breathing that facilitates a calmer and
wiser *bodily* approach to life than might otherwise
be the case. (I am not, of course, suggesting that all
people who pray, including me, are always calm or
wise, but the point is to make progress along the
way.) To sing prayerfully, then, is to invite a physical
transformation as well as to stand at the borderlands
of time and space.

Thus, the mere form of the Psalms – poems meant
to be sung – already points powerfully in the direction that, as I will suggest, the poems themselves are
determined to lead us.

In any case, the Psalms give every indication that
they stand intentionally at the intersection of God's

time and human time, with all the tensions that brings as well as the yearning for resolution. They stand deliberately on Mount Zion, where heaven and earth dangerously meet in the Temple, but they also look out into the whole creation. And they invite and facilitate that actual material transformation of the worshipper, of Israel as a whole, and of God's world as a whole, of which they sometimes speak.

Most of all, once more, they are designed as *worship:* the multidimensional worship in which every aspect of human life, love, fear, delight, anger, despair and gratitude is laid as an offering before the God who himself comes to stand at the crossroads of time, space and matter. The Psalms might not always seem to us particularly pure or worthy, as sacrifices should be. But I think part of the point is that they are *truthful,* the sincere outpourings of who and what the worshipper actually is. And when we worship the creator God with our whole, truthful self, we trust – and the Psalms strongly encourage this trust – that we will be remade. As Paul puts it, we are to be 're-newed in the image of the creator, bringing [us] into possession of new knowledge' (Col. 3.10).

All this points to the specifically Christian use of the Psalms. From the very beginning, the Christian church has seen the Psalms as containing, embodying and expressing a thousand hints and forward pointers to Jesus himself.

The reason the Psalms do this, however, is not simply so that a few verses here and there point forward across a void to events in the life of Jesus (Psalm 2 to his baptism, Psalm 22 to his crucifixion, Psalm 47 to his ascension, Psalm 72 to his rule of justice and peace over the whole world, and so on). No: they resonate with Jesus because he was the one who stood, by divine appointment, precisely at the intersection of God's time and ours, of God's space and ours, of God's matter and ours.

The distant memories and the long-range future hopes that the Psalms evoke and express came rushing together in the judgment and mercy of his life and death. The Temple, where the Psalms were sung, was an advance signpost to Jesus's sacrificial joining of heaven and earth. The Torah (which the Psalms celebrate), God's law that transforms the worshipper from the inside, was an advance signpost to his new way of life.

This is more, then, than simply saying that some psalms are to be seen as 'Christological', meaning either that some seem already to have been looking ahead to the coming of the ideal King or that some were read in that way by the early church. My point is deeper. I am suggesting that the entire worldview that the Psalms are inculcating was to do with that intersection of *our* time, space and matter with *God's*, which Christians believe happened uniquely and dramatically in Jesus.

In the same way, the *story* the Psalms tell is the story Jesus came to complete. It is the story of the creator God taking his power and reigning, ruling on earth as in heaven, delighting the whole creation by sorting out its messes and muddles, its injuries and injustices, once and for all. It is also the story of malevolent enemies prowling around, of people whispering lies and setting traps, and of sleepless nights and bottles full of tears.

Part of the strange work of the Psalms is to draw the terror and shame of all the ages together to a point where it becomes intense and unbearable, turning itself into a great scream of pain, the pain of Israel, the pain of Adam and Eve, the pain that shouts out, in the most paradoxical act of worship, to ask why God has abandoned it. And then of course the Psalms tell the story of strange vindication, of dramatic reversal, of wondrous rescue, comfort and restoration.

All these stories live together in the Psalms, side by side and frequently rolled into one. This isn't so much a matter of 'typology' – that's a matter of searching for patterns or 'typical' events in ancient scriptures that point forward to later ones. That may happen as well, but it's not what I'm talking about. Nor is it a matter of 'allegory', in which one speaks of one kind of 'reality' in order to point to a different one – though that often happens as well. It's a matter of learning to live within the great complex narrative that, with hindsight, Christians have discerned as the story of Jesus himself.

This kind of complex reading was controversial and difficult in the first century, and it remains so today. The early Christians clearly continued to use the Psalms in their own worship and prayer and (not least) in their theology. Most Jews did not believe that Jesus was Israel's Messiah, because they did not believe that he had been raised from the dead (the event that Jesus's followers regarded as having demonstrated his Messiahship, turning his crucifixion from a sign of failure into a means of victory). Most first-century

Jews, then, did not see things in the same way as Peter, Paul and the others. This wasn't, though, simply a matter of them disagreeing with half a dozen 'proof texts'. It was a larger issue altogether.

The notion of a large and complex story, which I mentioned earlier, had a lot to do with it. How could the story told by all the Psalms (not just the few obviously 'messianic' or 'Christological' ones) make sense? In Luke's Gospel, the risen Jesus explains to the puzzled and previously downcast disciples, 'Everything written about me in the law of Moses, and in the prophets and the Psalms, had to be fulfilled' (Lk. 24.44). This looks more like a way of reading the entire scriptural story, and within that the entire book of Psalms, than an attempt to pluck a few key texts out of a mass of otherwise unhelpful material.

Like all good poetry, then, the Psalms invite and sustain multiple levels of reading, but when we see them in the context of early Christianity, one level in particular stands out. The Psalter forms the great epic poem of the creator and covenant God who will at the last visit and redeem his people and, with them, his whole creation.

The early Christians believed that that was precisely what had happened in Jesus. The challenge of the Christian message is therefore not only the question that Jesus posed to his contemporaries and that, by his resurrection, he poses still. It is the challenge of a different way of understanding – and living within – the entire narrative.

It is perfectly possible to read or sing the Psalms without any such reference. That, of course, is what non-Christian Jews do to this day. But the Christian reading and singing of the Psalms is not simply a clever way of snatching a few helpful lines from someone else's hymnbook. Reading, praying and singing these poems as the prayer book that points to the Messiah himself makes a claim. It claims to inhabit the very heart of the Psalms, and the great and varied story they tell, in a way that nothing else quite does.

The Psalms thus exemplify and embody the actual 'authority' of scripture in its specifically Christian sense. (See *Scripture and the Authority of God* (SPCK, 2013).) Scripture is not simply a reference book to which we turn to look up correct answers – though it's full of those when we need them. Scripture is, at its heart, the great story that we sing in order not just to learn it with our heads but to become part of it through and through, the story that in turn becomes part of us. And if that is true of scripture as a whole (and, in the New Testament, of the Gospels as a whole), we might say that the very heart of scripture, working properly like this, is the book of Psalms.

Sing these songs, and they will renew you from head to toe, from heart to mind. Pray these poems, and they will sustain you on the long, hard but exhilarating road of Christian discipleship.

One final word before we press on. Paul speaks at one point of Christians as 'God's poem', God's 'artwork'. We are his 'workmanship', say some of the translations of Ephesians 2.10. The Greek word Paul uses there is *poiēma*, the very word from which the English word 'poem' is derived. God gives us these poems, the Psalms, as a gift, in order that through our praying and singing of them he may give *us* as a gift to his world. We are called to be living, breathing, praying, singing poems.

There are, of course, different types of poems. Some of us, perhaps, are sonnets. Some are haikus, or even limericks. Some are long, epic narrative poems. Some of us are in strict form, complete with rhymes. Some of us are in blank or free verse. The Psalms themselves come in many shapes and forms because

God wants people-poems of many shapes and forms. And he wants this rich variety so that through it all he may challenge the small and sterile imagination of his wider world. (See Ephesians 3.10.) The Psalms are not only poetry in themselves; they are to be the cause of poetry in those who sing them, together and individually. They are God's gifts to us so that we can be shaped as his gift to the world.

At both levels, this gift functions by transforming the *imagination*. It isn't so much that the world doesn't believe in God. Most people simply can't imagine what it might be like to live in God's world, in his time, in his space and in his matter. This book is aimed at helping God's people to imagine God's larger, richer world as they pray the Psalms. This is a wonderful thing to happen in itself. But it has a wider ultimate purpose: to enable the wider world, outside the church, to make that same leap of imagination as it sees what God's people are doing in the world and comes to realize that they are themselves poems that sing his praises. This is a large and ambitious goal. But with every psalm we sing we take another small step down that road.

Chapter 3

At the Threshold of God's Time

THE PSALMS INVITE US, FIRST, TO STAND AT THE
intersection of the different layers of time.

> *Lord, you have been our dwelling place*
>   *in all generations.*
> *Before the mountains were brought forth,*
>   *or ever you had formed the earth and the*
>   *world,*
>   *from everlasting to everlasting you*
>   *are God.*
> *You turn us back to dust,*
>   *and say, 'Turn back, you mortals.'*
> *For a thousand years in your sight*
>   *are like yesterday when it is past,*
>   *or like a watch in the night. (90.1–4)*

Compared with that, our sense of time is that it rushes past in a flash:

> For all our days pass away under your
>   wrath;
>   our years come to an end like a sigh.
> The days of our life are seventy years,
>   or perhaps eighty, if we are strong;
> even then their span is only toil and trouble;
>   they are soon gone, and we fly away.
>   (90.9–10)

All we can do, faced with this enormous discrepancy between God's time and ours, is to stand in awe and to pray:

> So teach us to count our days
>   that we may gain a wise heart. (90.12)

Make us, in other words, to be people who know how to stand at the threshold of human time and God's time, and there to learn both humility and hope. Our time is not worthless, but any worth it may possess will come from God's goodness, not our control of our circumstances:

Make us glad for as many days as you have
 afflicted us,
 and for as many years as we have seen
 evil.
Let your work be manifest to your servants,
 and your glorious power to their children.
Let the favour of the Lord our God be upon us,
 and prosper for us the work of our hands –
 O prosper the work of our hands!
 (90.15–17)

The same complex blend of lament, humility, resignation, and hope comes at the end of the long and sorrowful poem we know as Psalm 102. The radical difference between God's time and ours provides both the reason why we so often find ourselves perplexed at the course life takes and the reason why we can nevertheless find hope in the midst of it:

He has broken my strength in mid-course;
 he has shortened my days.
'O my God,' I say, 'do not take me away
 at the mid-point of my life,
you whose years endure
 throughout all generations.'

Long ago you laid the foundation of the
*   earth,*
*   and the heavens are the work of your*
*   hands.*
They will perish, but you endure;
*   they will all wear out like a garment.*
You change them like clothing, and they pass
*   away;*
*   but you are the same, and your years*
*   have no end.*
The children of your servants shall live
*   secure;*
*   their offspring shall be established in*
*   your presence. (102.23–28)*

If God is breaking our strength and shortening our days, we know that this is the same God who long ago laid the foundation of the earth, who will endure even though that earth might perish. He will be the same for ever, without end. In the same way, the great celebration of the next two psalms also speaks of the shortness of human time and the contrasting eternal love of God:

As for mortals, their days are like grass;
*   they flourish like a flower of the field;*

for the wind passes over it, and it is gone,
and its place knows it no more.
But the steadfast love of YHWH *is from*
everlasting to everlasting
on those who fear him,
and his righteousness to children's
children,
to those who keep his covenant
and remember to do his commandments.
(103.15–18)

Psalm 104 echoes this, describing how God hides his face and removes his breath from his creatures, and then sends forth his spirit so that they will be created once again:

When you hide your face, they are
dismayed;
when you take away their breath,
they die
and return to their dust.
When you send forth your spirit [or
'breath'], they are created;
and you renew the face of the ground.
(104.29–30)

All this appears to be teaching us to learn, some-how, the remarkable eschatological balance we see again and again, not only within individual psalms but in their ordering and juxtaposition within the book as a whole. Think, for example, of the balance be-tween the tub-thumping celebration of God's victory over Sihon, king of the Amorites, and Og, the king of Bashan, in Psalm 136 and the unrelieved sorrow and weeping by the waters of Babylon that immediately follow. Here is part of Psalm 136:

> [He] struck down great kings,
>> for his steadfast love endures for ever;
> and killed famous kings,
>> for his steadfast love endures for ever;
> Sihon, king of the Amorites,
>> for his steadfast love endures for ever;
> and Og, king of Bashan,
>> for his steadfast love endures for ever;
> and gave their land as a heritage,
>> for his steadfast love endures for ever;
> a heritage to his servant Israel,
>> for his steadfast love endures for ever.
>> (136.17–22)

And then here, at once, is the other side of the coin:

> *By the rivers of Babylon –*
> *there we sat down and there we wept*
> *when we remembered Zion. . . .*
> *How could we sing* YHWH's *song*
> *in a foreign land? (137.1, 4)*

This does not mean, of course, that the Psalms are inconsistent. This is the regular 'now and not yet' of the people of God, with all the emotions raw and (as usual in these poems) on the surface. The celebration is wild and uninhibited; the misery is deep and horrible. One moment we are chanting, perhaps clapping our hands in time, even stamping our feet; Psalm 136 reminds me of the kind of song boys might sing on the bus on the way back from a victorious soccer game. The next moment we have tears running down our cheeks, and we want the earth to open and swallow us. (We shouldn't miss the extra point here. It may be impossible to 'sing YHWH's song' in this foreign land, but this particular psalmist turns this impossibility itself into yet another of 'YHWH's songs', thus making a psalm out of the fact that one can't sing psalms here. If that reminds us of Israel's greatest prophet sensing himself utterly abandoned by God and yet still able to ask God why he has abandoned him, that is probably part of the point.)

To recognize that the Psalms call us to pray and sing at the intersection of the times – of our time and God's time, of the *then* and the *now* and the *not yet* – is to understand how those emotions are to be held within the rhythm of a life lived in God's presence.

In particular, the theme of time helps us with those great and central psalms that celebrate the installation and victory of God's chosen king. From the opening of Psalm 2 through the other royal moments in Psalms 18, 20, and 21; in 45 and 61; to the majestic 72; the short and startling 110; and the discursive 132; this is a theme that we can't do without but that often, in our culture, we don't know what to do *with*.

How does a Christian, not least a modern Christian who values our developed Western democracy, pray these lines?

> *I will tell of the decree of* YHWH:
> *He said to me, 'You are my son;*
> *today I have begotten you.*

Ask of me, and I will make the nations your
heritage,
    and the ends of the earth your possession.
You shall break them with a rod of iron,
    and dash them in pieces like a potter's
    vessel.'
Now therefore, O kings, be wise;
    be warned, O rulers of the earth.
Serve YHWH with fear,
    with trembling kiss his feet,
or he will be angry, and you will perish in
    the way;
    for his wrath is quickly kindled.
Happy are all who take refuge in him.
    (2.7–12)

For you girded me with strength for the
    battle;
    you made my assailants sink under
    me. . . .
They cried for help, but there was no one to
    save them;
    they cried to YHWH, but he did not
    answer them.
I beat them fine, like dust before the wind;

I cast them out like the mire of the
  streets. . . .
People whom I had not known
  served me.
As soon as they heard of me they obeyed me;
  foreigners came cringing to me. . . .
For this I will extol you, O YHWH, *among the*
  nations,
  and sing praises to your name.
Great triumphs he gives to his king,
  and shows steadfast love to his anointed,
  to David and his descendants for ever.
    (18.39, 41–44, 49–50)

For the king trusts in YHWH,
  and through the steadfast love of the
    Most High he shall not be moved.
Your hand will find out all your enemies;
  your right hand will find out those who
    hate you.
You will make them like a fiery furnace
  when you appear.
YHWH *will swallow them up in his wrath,*
  and fire will consume them.
You will destroy their offspring from the
  earth,

and their children from among
   humankind. (21.7–10)

YHWH *says to my lord,*
'Sit at my right hand
   until I make your enemies your
      footstool.'
YHWH *sends out from Zion*
   your mighty sceptre.
   Rule in the midst of your foes. . . .
The Lord is at your right hand;
   he will shatter kings on the day of his
      wrath.
He will execute judgement among the nations,
   filling them with corpses;
he will shatter heads
   over the wide earth. (110.1–2, 5–6)

These are among the more obviously (and, to us, worryingly) violent of the 'royal' psalms. But even those that offer a more peaceful scene have disturbed many in our day through their lofty assumption of a monarchical rule that will bring the nations of the world into submission:

Give the king your justice, O God,
   and your righteousness to a king's son.
May he judge your people with
       righteousness,
   and your poor with justice.
May the mountains yield prosperity for the
       people,
   and the hills, in righteousness.
May he defend the cause of the poor of the
       people,
give deliverance to the needy,
   and crush the oppressor.
May he live while the sun endures,
   and as long as the moon, throughout all
       generations. . . .
May he have dominion from sea to sea,
   and from the River to the ends of the
       earth.
May his foes bow down before him,
   and his enemies lick the dust.
May the kings of Tarshish and of the isles
   render him tribute,
may the kings of Sheba and Seba
   bring gifts.
May all kings fall down before him,

all nations give him service.
(72.1–5, 8–11)

Granted, the psalm goes on at once to describe the way in which the (ideal) king will deliver the needy when they call, and come to the aid of the poor and helpless, taking pity on the weak and the needy and rescuing them from oppression and violence (72.12–14). Despite this, many in our democratic age have taken exception to the extraordinary exaltation that the psalm claims for the king. Can it really be appropriate to say this of any human ruler?

May his name endure for ever,
  his fame continue as long as the sun.
May all nations be blessed in him;
  may they pronounce him happy. (72.17)

Haven't these psalms, and the others like 149 that go with them, been used and abused to justify tyranny and wickedness? Yes, of course – just as the soft and meditative psalms have been used to justify quietistic retreat from God's world; the penitential psalms have been used to justify endless overscrupulous navel-gazing; and the celebrations of creation have been used to express a soggy, romantic pantheism. The abuse doesn't remove the use. But what is 'the use' in this case? What are these royal psalms celebrating? How can we sing them today?

To understand this, we have to take a step backwards – actually, two or three steps. The Psalms, all of them and not least these royal ones, mean what they mean within the larger worldview that (if we may generalize for a moment) scripture as a whole articulates. It goes something like this:

God created humans in the beginning to be his vice-rulers over the world. That is part, at least, of what it meant that humans were made 'in God's image'. The 'image' is like an angled mirror, reflecting God's wise and caring love into the world, bringing order and fruitfulness to the garden where the humans were placed. That project was, of course, tragically twisted with human arrogance and sin. But it has never been rescinded.

Indeed, though the psalmists were as aware as anyone of the darkness within every human heart, Psalm 8 can still gloriously remind us of the human vocation. In the old Book of Common Prayer version, where 'man' denoted 'human being', it asks, wonderingly,

What is man, that thou art mindful of him:
And the son of man, that thou visitest him?
Thou madest him lower than the angels:
To crown him with glory and worship.
Thou makest him to have dominion of the
works of thy hands:
And thou hast put all things in subjection
under his feet. (8.4–6)

This does not make human beings 'masters of creation' in an arrogant or tyrannical sense. The psalm begins and ends with a glad shout of praise: 'O Lord our Governor: how excellent is thy Name in all the world!' (8.1, 9).

When humans take up their divinely appointed role, looking after God's world on his behalf, this is not a Promethean attempt to usurp God's role. It is the humble, obedient carrying out of the role that has been assigned. The real arrogance would be to refuse the vocation, imagining that we knew better than God the purpose for which we have been put here.

But there is then a further vocation, one that has routinely been forgotten throughout much of church history. In the Bible, God not only called human beings to look after creation. He also called Israel to be the means of rescuing the world from the plight into which it had fallen.

God's call of Abraham echoes the vocation of Adam: 'Be fruitful and multiply' in Genesis 1.28 turns into 'I will make you exceedingly numerous . . . I will make you exceedingly fruitful' in Genesis 17.2, 6. And whereas the story of Genesis 3–11 is one of disaster, curse, and continuing human arrogance, the story that begins in Genesis 12 with God's call of Abraham has for its motto the promise, 'In you all the families of the earth shall be blessed' (v. 3). This theme continues in one way or another in many parts of the Old Testament.

The significance of this cannot be overestimated. God created the world in such a way that it was to be looked after by humans who reflect his image. When the humans rebelled, he did not rescind that project. Instead, he called a human family in order that they might reflect not simply his wise ordering and stewardship into the world but now also his rescuing love into that same world, disastrously flawed as it now was. Here is the ecstasy and the agony of the Old Testament: the rich, breathtaking vocation of Israel and the dark, tragic fact that this vocation, this rescue mission, was to be undertaken by a people who were themselves in sore need of the very same rescue.

The darkness and puzzle of this double theme is reflected in every book of the Old Testament and is seen right across the Psalter. Just as the human rebellion did not cause God to abandon the project to bring his order into creation through humans (Psalm 8), so Israel's constant and humiliating failure did not cause God to abandon the project to rescue the world through his chosen people. That is surely the message of the great historical psalms and the sidelong references to that same history elsewhere:

> *Give ear, O my people, to my teaching;*
>> *incline your ears to the words of my*
>>> *mouth. . . .*
> *We will tell to the coming generation*
> *the glorious deeds of* YHWH, *and his might,*
>> *and the wonders that he has done. . . .*
> *That they should not be like their ancestors,*
>> *a stubborn and rebellious generation,*
> *a generation whose heart was not steadfast,*
>> *whose spirit was not faithful to God.*
> *The Ephraimites, armed with the bow,*
>> *turned back on the day of battle.*

They did not keep God's covenant,
  but refused to walk according to his law.
They forgot what he had done,
  and the miracles that he had shown them. . . .
Yet they sinned still more against him,
  rebelling against the Most High in the
    desert.
They tested God in their heart
  by demanding the food they craved. . . .
Therefore, when YHWH *heard, he was full of*
    rage;
  a fire was kindled against Jacob,
  his anger mounted against Israel,
because they had no faith in God,
  and did not trust his saving power.
    (78.1, 4, 8–11, 17–18, 21–22; the whole
    long psalm continues the same theme)

And whereas Psalm 105 celebrates God's choice of Abraham and his family, and his deliverance of them from slavery in Egypt, Psalm 106 immediately goes on to tell the dark side of the same story:

Both we and our ancestors have sinned;
  we have committed iniquity, have done
    wickedly.

Our ancestors, when they were in Egypt,
  did not consider your wonderful works;
they did not remember the abundance of
      your steadfast love,
    but rebelled against the Most High at the
      Red Sea. . . .
But they soon forgot his works;
  they did not wait for his counsel.
But they had a wanton craving in the
    wilderness,
    and put God to the test in the desert. . . .
They made a calf at Horeb
and worshipped a cast image.
They exchanged the glory of God
  for the image of an ox that eats grass.
They forgot God, their Saviour,
  who had done great things in Egypt,
wondrous works in the land of Ham,
  and awesome deeds by the Red Sea.
    (106.6–7, 13–14, 19–22)

Nor does this rebellion stop when Israel reaches the
promised land at last:

They did not destroy the peoples
  as YHWH *commanded them,*

but they mingled with the nations
*   and learned to do as they did.*
They served their idols,
*   which became a snare to them.*
They sacrificed their sons
*   and their daughters to the demons;*
they poured out innocent blood,
*   the blood of their sons and daughters,*
whom they sacrificed to the idols of Canaan;
*   and the land was polluted with blood.*
Thus they became unclean by their acts,
*   and prostituted themselves in their*
*   doings. (106.34–39)*

Nevertheless, several psalms continue to celebrate the divine call to Israel and the providential protection that has preserved the nation despite everything. These focus, often enough, on Jerusalem and the Temple. A good example is 118, frequently quoted in the New Testament:

All nations surrounded me;
*   in the name of YHWH I cut them off!*
They surrounded me, surrounded me on
*   every side;*
*   in the name of YHWH I cut them off!*

They surrounded me like bees;
   they blazed like a fire of thorns;
   in the name of YHWH *I cut them off!*
I was pushed hard, so that I was falling,
   but YHWH *helped me.*
YHWH *is my strength and my might;*
   he has become my salvation. . . .
Open to me the gates of righteousness,
   that I may enter through them
   and give thanks to YHWH.
This is the gate of YHWH;
   the righteous shall enter through it.
I thank you that you have answered me
   and have become my salvation.
The stone that the builders rejected
   has become the chief cornerstone.
This is YHWH's *doing;*
   it is marvellous in our eyes.
This is the day that YHWH *has made;*
   let us rejoice and be glad in it.
         (118.10–14, 19–24)

Sometimes the celebration is straightforward, telling the story of the Exodus and insisting that YHWH is completely different from the idols of the nations. Even there, however, as in 135, there is a note not merely of triumph at past victories but of trust for future ones, implying that Israel will still need rescuing:

> *Your name, O* YHWH, *endures for ever,*
> *your renown, O* YHWH, *throughout all*
> *ages.*
> *For* YHWH *will vindicate his people,*
> *And have compassion on his servants.*
> *(135.13–14)*

And as we have already noted, the tub-thumping 136 is followed at once by the heart-stopping 137: we move straight from celebrating the victory of God, 'for his steadfast love endures for ever', to 'By the rivers of Babylon – there we sat down and there we wept.'

This double-edged memory is echoed in single verses, such as 99.8:

> *O* YHWH *our God, you answered them;*
> *you were a forgiving God to them,*
> *but an avenger of their wrongdoings.*

We may wonder at this combination: What does it mean that God both forgave them *and* punished them? Perhaps the answer is that the sinners among Israel received their just recompense but that the vocation of Israel as a whole was renewed. Even though the nation went through terrible times, up to and including the exile itself, poets and prophets refused to believe that God had abandoned it or that his purpose for it would now come to an end. When it seems as though that has happened, the psalmists look back to God's mighty deeds of old and claim them as the pattern of what will happen in the future as well:

> *I cry aloud to God,*
>   *aloud to God, that he may hear me. . . .*
> *'Will the Lord spurn for ever,*
>   *and never again be favourable?*
> *Has his steadfast love ceased for ever?*
>   *Are his promises at an end for all time?*
> *Has God forgotten to be gracious?*
>   *Has he in anger shut up his*
>   *compassion?' . . .*
> *I will call to mind the deeds of* YHWH;
>   *I will remember your wonders of old.*
> *I will meditate on all your work,*
>   *and muse on your mighty deeds. . . .*
> *When the waters saw you, O God,*

when the waters saw you, they were
afraid;
the very deep trembled.
The clouds poured out water;
the skies thundered;
your arrows flashed on every side.
The crash of your thunder was in the
whirlwind;
your lightnings lit up the world;
the earth trembled and shook.
Your way was through the sea,
your path, through the mighty waters;
yet your footprints were unseen.
You led your people like a flock
by the hand of Moses and Aaron.
(77.1, 7–9, 11–12, 16–20)

Again and again, it is God's powerful rescue of his people in the Exodus that provides the template: the sign of what his power can do, and the pledge that it will happen again when Israel needs it. Look at his deeds, declares the psalmist to the world of creation, and tremble:

Tremble, O earth, at the presence of YHWH,
at the presence of the God of Jacob,

who turns the rock into a pool of water,
  the flint into a spring of water. (114.7–8)

All this is not simply a repeated assertion of national superiority, made in the teeth of the all-too-obvious national failures. It is a repeated assertion of the divine purpose, not only *for* Israel but *through* Israel. These psalms look beyond the present time to the coming time. More specifically, they look back to the great moments of the *past* in order to frame the pain and puzzlement of the *present* within the hope that God will one day do again, in the *future*, what he did long ago, and thus enable Israel to fulfil its long-promised role in the end.

Now, at last, we come to the central point. Here is the larger framework: God calls humans to be his rulers over creation, and though humans have distorted this vocation into ugly parodies, treating God's creation as if it were a mere toy to play with or resource to exploit, God has not rescinded the project or the vocation.

Here is the narrower framework: God calls Israel, a human family, to be his rescue operation for the world, and though Israel has distorted this vocation and used this opportunity to bite the hand that feeds it, and to worship other gods instead of him, God has not rescinded the project or the vocation.

But now, within the sharp focus of both frameworks, God calls David, a human being after God's own heart, the one who will sum up the task and vocation of Israel in himself. It is to David, or more specifically David's son and heir, that the task has now devolved of bringing the nations into submission to Israel's God, the creator.

The psalms we noted before, such as 2, 18, 21, 72, and 110, are not random exaltations of a militaristic monarch. They express, in the language and idiom of the time, the conviction that it is through the coming king (the human one, Israel's anointed representative) that YHWH will establish his rule on earth as in heaven.

Here, too, the psalmists, taken as a whole, acknowledge that the present kings can and do fail, and fail horribly. David himself was deeply flawed. Psalm 51 stands near the heart of this sequence, showing graphically that the person upon whom these large purposes rest must himself go through humiliation and repentance. There is no consensus as to when the headings were added to the Psalms, but certainly well before the time of Jesus Psalm 51 was seen as the prayer of penitence, which David offered after his adultery with Bathsheba and his murder of her husband, Uriah:

Have mercy on me, O God,
  according to your steadfast love;
according to your abundant mercy
  blot out my transgressions.
Wash me thoroughly from my iniquity,
  and cleanse me from my sin.
For I know my transgressions,
  and my sin is ever before me.
Against you, you alone, have I sinned,
  and done what is evil in your sight,
so that you are justified in your sentence
  and blameless when you pass judgement.
    (51.1–4)

Humans have sinned, but God will still work through them; Israel has sinned, but God will still use its people to bless the nations; monarchs have sinned grievously, but God still promises to bring the world into subjection under his anointed king. Unless this is sheer folly on God's part, or indeed sheer arrogance on the psalmist's part, this can only mean that these songs are to be sung in the light of God's intended future.

Someday, somehow, there will come a time when a Davidic king will be exalted over the nations and bring God's justice and peace to the world. And part of the task of that coming king will be, somehow, to take upon himself not only the role of ruling Israel and the world but of bringing to its head the long history of failure – human failure, Israel's failure, royal history. The prophets, especially Isaiah, point to all this as well.

And, as in Isaiah, the Psalms seem to indicate that this long-awaited promise can and will only be fulfilled through a time of intense suffering. It is hard to tell whether the 'suffering' psalms are also intended to be 'royal', though some have thought so. The sequence of thought in the great Psalm 22 does seem to indicate this as a possibility, moving from the God-forsaken lament at the start to the glorious vision of the kingdom at the end:

> *My God, my God, why have you*
> *forsaken me?*
> *Why are you so far from helping me,*
> *from the words of my groaning?*

O my God, I cry by day, but you do not
　　answer;
　and by night, but find no rest. . . .
But I am a worm, and not human;
　scorned by others, and despised by the
　　people.
All who see me mock at me;
　they make mouths at me, they shake
　　their heads. . . .
I am poured out like water,
　and all my bones are out of joint;
my heart is like wax;
　it is melted within my breast;
my mouth is dried up like a potsherd,
　and my tongue sticks to my jaws;
　you lay me in the dust of death.
　　(22.1–2, 6–7, 14–15)

And then, quite suddenly, the shout of triumph:

I will tell of your name to my brothers and
　　sisters;
　in the midst of the congregation I will
　　praise you:
You who fear YHWH, praise him!
　All you offspring of Jacob, glorify him;

stand in awe of him, all you offspring of
   Israel! . . .
All the ends of the earth shall remember
   and turn to YHWH;
and all the families of the nations
   shall worship before him.
For dominion belongs to YHWH,
   and he rules over the nations.
      (22.22–23, 27–28)

Taken individually, then, one might indeed read psalms such as 2 or 110 as over-triumphalist. But the Psalter as we have it insists on our reading them within the larger context in which all ordinary kings are to face the challenge of their own inadequacy or worse. Penitence here, suffering there; only so will the larger promises be fulfilled.

This doesn't nullify the glorious statements of Psalm 2: that God will give his royal son the nations for his inheritance and the uttermost parts of the world for his possession. Paul picks up exactly that promise in Romans 8.17–26. It doesn't take away the grand sweep of Psalm 72, that the king's dominion will be from one sea to the other, from the River to the ends of the earth. And this theme can, of course, only be fully understood when we trace the lines forward and see them meeting in Jesus's baptism, in his royal inauguration of God's kingdom, then not least in Gethsemane and on the cross, with Psalm 22 coming into its own both as a terrifying lament ('My God, my God, why did you abandon me?' Matt. 27.46 / Mark 15.34) and then as the reaffirmation of God's kingdom, opening up on the other side of the psalm into the new day in which he will be enthroned over all the nations.

When we take the Psalms as a whole and learn to stand at their complex intersection of God's time and ours, of the past Davidic kingdom with its flaws and failures and the coming kingdom of God, with Jesus at the middle of that sequence, we find that they themselves express the eschatological tension and invite us to stand exactly there.

Nowhere is this better seen than in Psalm 89. The promises and the present situation are placed side by side, together forming a massive and poetically majestic question mark. The only way the writer dares approach the terror of the present is through the trustworthy promises of the past. The prayer at the end is simply that YHWH will 'remember'.

And we note, in parallel with some other statements of the terrible things that God's people have
to face, that here the psalmist will not say that an
enemy, or even some other god, is responsible for
what has happened. No: *You* have done it. *You* have
rejected David, *you* have renounced the covenant,
you have exalted the king's enemies:

> *I will sing of your steadfast love, O* YHWH,
>   *for ever;*
>   *with my mouth I will proclaim your*
>   *faithfulness to all generations.*
> *I declare that your steadfast love is*
>   *established for ever;*
>   *your faithfulness is as firm as the*
>   *heavens.*
> *You said, 'I have made a covenant with my*
>   *chosen one,*
>   *I have sworn to my servant David:*
> *"I will establish your descendants for ever,*
>   *and build your throne for all*
>   *generations." '. . .*
> *Then you spoke in a vision to your faithful*
>   *one, and said:*
> *'I have set the crown on one who is mighty,*

I have exalted one chosen from the
>> *people.*
I have found my servant David;
>> *with my holy oil I have anointed him;*
my hand shall always remain with him;
>> *my arm also shall strengthen him. . . .*
He shall cry to me, "You are my Father,
>> *my God, and the Rock of my salvation!"*
I will make him the firstborn,
>> *the highest of the kings of the earth.*
For ever I will keep my steadfast love for him,
>> *and my covenant with him will stand*
>> *firm.*
I will establish his line for ever,
>> *and his throne as long as the heavens*
>> *endure. . . .*
I will not violate my covenant,
>> *or alter the word that went forth from*
>> *my lips.*
Once and for all I have sworn by my
>> *holiness;*
>> *I will not lie to David.*
His line shall continue for ever,
>> *and his throne endure before me like*
>> *the sun.*

It shall be established for ever like the moon,
an enduring witness in the skies.'
(89.1–4, 19–21, 26–29, 34–37)

And then, without warning:

But now you have spurned and rejected him;
you are full of wrath against your
anointed.
You have renounced the covenant with your
servant;
you have defiled his crown in the dust.
You have broken through all his walls;
you have laid his strongholds in
ruins. . . .
You have removed the sceptre from his hand,
and hurled his throne to the ground.
You have cut short the days of his youth;
you have covered him with shame.
(89.38–40, 44–45)

All that the poet can then do is ask the question and
beg that YHWH will 'remember':

How long, O YHWH? Will you hide yourself
for ever?

How long will your wrath burn like fire?
Remember how short my time is –
   for what vanity you have created all
      mortals!
Who can live and never see death?
   Who can escape the power of Sheol?
Lord, where is your steadfast love of old,
   which by your faithfulness you swore to
      David?
Remember, O Lord, how your servant is
      taunted;
   how I bear in my bosom the insults of the
      peoples,
with which your enemies taunt, O YHWH,
   with which they taunted the footsteps of
      your anointed. (89.46–51)

One may assume that the concluding verse ('Blessed be YHWH for ever. Amen and Amen') was added later. In the final editing and collection of all these poems, Psalm 89 is the end of 'Book III' of the five 'Books' into which they are divided; someone undoubtedly decided that the section needed a more solid final note.

But it should not be thought inappropriate. Job, after all, continues to bless the name of YHWH in the midst of his disasters. This concluding benediction is simply a way of holding the whole puzzling and frightening story together. It goes with the repeated 'you' of verses 38–45 (which echoes the repeated 'you' in the psalm immediately before this one – Psalm 88, the darkest poem in the whole book). It is a way of holding on to God in the darkness, even when – precisely when! – the problem is that God seems to have gone back on his word, to have abandoned his promises and his people, and particularly to have forgotten his specific promises to the king himself. The psalm offers a way of continuing to worship without pretence, eyes open to the terrible reality.

This is what poetry and music themselves are there to do: to link the present to the past, to say, 'Remember', to say, 'Blessed be God', even when the tide is running strongly in the wrong direction.

The psalm insists that God must and will remind himself, as the singers remind themselves, of the larger story. Go back, says the poet, and see where it all started; look ahead and remember where you've promised that this story will end. And, says the psalmist, as we stand in perplexity at the intersections of past, present and future, so, YHWH, will you remember – remember how short our time is (v. 47), remember your steadfast love of old (v. 49), and remember what the enemies have done (vv. 50–51). Just remember. Bring the past into the present, and that will sustain us as we wait in the dark for your future.

All this, it seems to me, apart from any sidelong reference to Jesus himself, would be readily understood by a second-Temple Jew used to hundreds of years of disappointed hopes and false dawns, but with a memory as long as the covenant and a hope that refused to die. The hope was expressed in many ways but in particular in the theme of God's restorative justice. Future judgment does, of course, have a punitive element, but that is the necessarily negative side of God's project to restore not only Israel but the whole creation.

Again and again this comes through, not least in those great psalms 96 and 98. We can somehow stand firm in the present because YHWH is coming – coming to judge the earth; he will judge it with righteousness, and the peoples with his truth. The trees and the fields, the seas and the floods will celebrate it, and we as humans do so in advance.

So this future glance turns into prayer: Arise, O God; don't just lie there all afternoon. Get up and do something! (See Pss. 68.1; 74.22.) That prayer of impatience is precisely what happens when we are caught at the intersection of the times. We can imagine devout second-Temple Jews praying like that. And as we join in their prayer, we catch our breath as we come forward to a small boat on the Sea of Galilee and hear the disciples saying more or less the same thing to the sleeping Jesus while the winds and storms are raging all around. 'We're going down! Don't you care?' (Mark 4.38).

We are given those psalms, I believe, so that we can pray them ourselves out of our own impatience. God in his wisdom knows that we shall want and need to express the pain of being caught in the crack of time. We have seen God incarnate rise up from his three days' sleep to be enthroned as judge of the world. Yet we still await the final fulfilment of Psalms 2, 8, and 110 – psalms that both Paul and Hebrews used to express their view of Jesus in the present and their hope for his future coming as judge. There really will come a time when people will say, 'Surely there is a God who judges on earth' (Psalm 58.11). Our confidence in the future restorative justice of God may even give us confidence to do justice ourselves in the present (Ps. 75.10).

We are called, then, to stretch out the arms of our minds and hearts, and to find ourselves, Christ-shaped, cross-shaped, at the intersection of the past, present, and future of God's time and our own time. This is a place of intense pain and intense joy, the sort that perhaps only music and poetry can express or embody. The Psalms are gifts that help us not only to think wisely about the overlaps and paradoxes of time, but to live within them, to reach out in the day of trouble and remind ourselves – and not only ourselves, but also the mysterious one whom the Psalms call 'you' – of the story in which we live. Past, present and future belong to him. We are called to live, joyfully and painfully, in the story that is both his and ours. Our times are in his hand.

Chapter 4

Where God Dwells

THE MYSTERY OF SPACE AND PLACE IN THE
Psalms hits us in the face when we stop for a moment
and remind ourselves what they are saying. The first
time I went to Jerusalem, I lived for some months at
St George's Cathedral, a few minutes' walk from the
Damascus Gate at the north side of the Old City. Day
by day, at the cathedral, we said or sang the Psalms;
and suddenly, in that geographical context, I realized
how apparently absurd they sound.

Again and again the Psalms celebrate, in almost
embarrassingly vivid language, the belief that the
creator of the universe has, for reasons best known
to him, decided to take up residence on a small hill
in the Judean uplands. The living God, the Psalms
declare, has decided to make his own special home

at the point where the fertile western escarpment meets the eastern wilderness. It is poised between garden and desert – almost as though God couldn't quite make up his mind whether to settle firmly in a New Eden or to remain camped with his people in their wilderness wanderings.

In David's mind's eye, at least, Jerusalem was designed to be seen as the place where, at last, Israel's God would cease his wandering and dwell in one place. Deciding on this previously unconquered city as his new capital, David was playing a shrewd political move. No one tribe would be able to claim that YHWH had picked out one of *their* cities as his very own (though David's own family, the tribe of Judah, would quickly come to make that connection).

No doubt all this produced theological tensions with the Pentateuchal traditions of the constantly moving tabernacle. Was God really going to be found in one place? How would one avoid the danger of idolatry?

No doubt the dangers of arrogance and the concentration of power were there from the start, as we see already in the story of Solomon, never mind his successors, and in the constant critique of the prophets. Yet the Zion traditions in the Psalms are not to be pushed aside as so much mistaken ideology. They express, in a way that only those prepared to live at the intersection of the times will understand, the intersection of space: of God's space with our space, of heaven with earth.

This is the point that Western modernity regards as so incomprehensible as to be laughable: the eternal creator coming to live at one point on the earth?

Within classic philosophies, either the gods are far away in their own heaven and don't get involved, as in Epicureanism, or they are omnipresent in a pantheistic world, as in Stoicism. Maybe, in ordinary ancient paganism, some gods or goddesses might decide to live or act in one place rather than another. Athene, obviously, lived in Athens; Artemis, less obviously but equally powerfully, lived in Ephesus. But to suggest that the world's sovereign creator might live in one place – well, it was not only philosophically ridiculous but also politically dangerous.

That was part of the point. Once you say that the world's creator lives in Jerusalem, you are going to go on to say – and the Psalms regularly do go on to say – that from Jerusalem he will rule all the nations. Jerusalem is not the place where God's people go to be in a safe retreat, away from the rest of the world. The living God establishes his throne in Zion so that from there his judgment will go out to all the nations:

> *The kings of the earth set themselves,*
>> *and the rulers take counsel together,*
>> *against YHWH and his anointed, saying,*
> *'Let us burst their bonds asunder,*
>> *and cast their cords from us.'*
> *He who sits in the heavens laughs;*
>> *YHWH has them in derision.*
> *Then he will speak to them in his wrath,*
>> *and terrify them in his fury, saying,*
> *'I have set my king on Zion, my holy*
>> *hill.' . . .*
> *Now therefore, O kings, be wise;*
>> *be warned, O rulers of the earth.*
> *Serve YHWH with fear,*
>> *with trembling kiss his feet.*
>> *(2.2–6, 10–12)*

Or again, with a message of comfort but no less emphatically:

> *Sing praises to YHWH, who dwells in Zion.*
>> *Declare his deeds among the peoples.*

For he who avenges blood is mindful of
    them;
he does not forget the cry of the afflicted.
    (9.11–12)

Zion, the hill of YHWH, is the place from which he will hear his people's prayer and come to their rescue (Ps. 3.4; compare 1 Kings 8.22–53). When they are away from it, they will be sad, missing that sense of divine presence, and will long to return:

My soul is cast down within me;
    therefore I remember you
from the land of Jordan and of Hermon,
    from Mount Mizar. . . .
O send out your light and your truth;
    let them lead me;
let them bring me to your holy hill
    and to your dwelling.
Then I will go to the altar of God,
    to God my exceeding joy;
and I will praise you with the harp,
    O God, my God.
        (42.6; 43.3–4 [Pss. 42 and 43
        together form a single poem])

It is a place that demands a holiness from Israel that
will match YHWH's own:

> O YHWH, *who may abide in your tent?*
>> *Who may dwell on your holy hill?*
> *Those who walk blamelessly, and do what is*
>>> *right,*
>> *and speak the truth from their heart.*
>>> *(15.1–2)*

> *Who shall ascend the hill of YHWH?*
>> *And who shall stand in his holy place?*
> *Those who have clean hands and pure*
>>> *hearts,*
>> *who do not lift up their souls to what is*
>> *false,*
>> *and do not swear deceitfully.*
> *They will receive blessing from YHWH,*
>> *and vindication from the God of their*
>>> *salvation. (24.3–5)*

Psalm 48 deserves to be quoted in full for its poetic
sweep. It begins and ends with a celebration of Zion
and of God's abiding and effectual presence within
it, and holds within that framework, first, the over-

throw of the kingdoms of the earth and, second, the pondering of God's love and victory by his people. Thus the poem begins with the celebration:

> *Great is YHWH and greatly to be praised*
> *in the city of our God.*
> *His holy mountain, beautiful in elevation,*
> *is the joy of all the earth,*
> *Mount Zion, in the far north,*
> *the city of the great King.*
> *Within its citadels God*
> *has shown himself a sure defence.*
> *(48.1–3)*

So what happens when the rulers of the earth come to make war against Zion? As Psalm 2 had warned, they are overthrown:

> *Then the kings assembled,*
> *they came on together.*
> *As soon as they saw it, they were*
> *astounded;*
> *they were in panic, they took to flight;*
> *trembling took hold of them there,*
> *pains as of a woman in labour,*

as when an east wind shatters
    the ships of Tarshish.
As we have heard, so have we seen
    in the city of YHWH *of hosts,*
in the city of our God,
    which God establishes for ever. (48.4–8)

God's people can therefore pause and celebrate his rescuing love:

We ponder your steadfast love, O God,
    in the midst of your temple.
Your name, O God, like your praise,
    reaches to the ends of the earth.
Your right hand is filled with victory.
    Let Mount Zion be glad,
let the towns of Judah rejoice
    because of your judgements. (48.9–11)

The people, in other words, have been observing the way in which the promise of verses 1–3 have in fact been fulfilled in the events of verses 4–8. This then leads to their responsibility to alert future generations to the same point:

Walk about Zion, go all around it,
  count its towers,
consider well its ramparts;
  go through its citadels,
that you may tell the next generation
  that this is God,
our God for ever and ever.
  He will be our guide for ever. *(48.12–14)*

The same point is celebrated in psalms such as 76:

In Judah God is known,
  his name is great in Israel.
His abode has been established in Salem,
  his dwelling-place in Zion.
There he broke the flashing arrows,
  the shield, the sword, and the weapons
    of war.
Glorious are you, more majestic
  than the everlasting mountains.
The stout-hearted were stripped of their spoil;
  they sank into sleep;
none of the troops
  was able to lift a hand.
At your rebuke, O God of Jacob,

> *both rider and horse lay stunned.*
> *(76.1–6)*

The same theme occurs again and again in the great crescendo of praise that moves through the collection between Psalms 95 and 100:

> *Ascribe to* YHWH*, O families of the peoples,*
> *ascribe to* YHWH *glory and strength.*
> *Ascribe to* YHWH *the glory due his name;*
> *bring an offering, and come into his*
> *courts.*
> *Worship* YHWH *in holy splendour;*
> *tremble before him, all the earth.*
> *(96.7–9)*

> *The heavens proclaim his righteousness;*
> *and all the peoples behold his glory.*
> *All worshippers of images are put to shame,*
> *those who make their boast in worthless*
> *idols;*
> *all gods bow down before him.*
> *Zion hears and is glad,*
> *and the towns of Judah rejoice,*
> *because of your judgements, O God.*

For you, O YHWH, are most high over all the
  earth;
  you are exalted far above all gods.
  (97.6–9)

YHWH is king; let the peoples tremble!
  He sits enthroned upon the cherubim; let
    the earth quake!
YHWH is great in Zion;
  he is exalted over all the peoples.
  (99.1–2)

This, of course, is why the pilgrim psalms, the
Songs of Ascents, traditionally known as the songs
to be sung by pilgrims on their way up to Jerusalem
for the great festivals, are what they are. Jerusalem
and the Temple itself are not just a convenient gathering point: they are the place of promise, the place
of presence, the place out of all the earth where the
living God has chosen to live:

I was glad when they said to me,
  'Let us go to the house of YHWH!'
Our feet are standing
  within your gates, O Jerusalem.

Jerusalem – built as a city
 that is bound firmly together.
To it the tribes go up,
 the tribes of YHWH,
as was decreed for Israel,
 to give thanks to the name of YHWH.
For there the thrones for judgement were
  set up,
 the thrones of the house of David.
 (122.1–5)

And then, in a lovely piece of poetic alliteration, the poet exploits the verbal link between 'Jeru-salem' and the words for 'pray' (*sha'al*) and for 'peace' (*shalōm*). 'Pray for the peace of Jerusalem,' he says (*Sha'alu shalōm Yerushalaim*):

Pray for the peace of Jerusalem:
 'May they prosper who love you.
Peace be within your walls,
 and security within your towers.'
For the sake of my relatives and friends
 I will say, 'Peace be within you.'
For the sake of the house of YHWH our God,
 I will seek your good. (122.6–9)

Once again there is balance: first, in Psalm 125, we are invited to celebrate the absolute security of Mount Zion, but then, in Psalm 126, we are invited to celebrate the restoration of Jerusalem after the terrible disaster of exile:

> *Those who trust in* YHWH *are like Mount*
> *Zion,*
> *which cannot be moved, but abides*
> *for ever.*
> *As the mountains surround Jerusalem,*
> *so* YHWH *surrounds his people,*
> *from this time on and for evermore.*
> *For the sceptre of wickedness shall not rest*
> *on the land allotted to the righteous,*
> *so that the righteous might not stretch out*
> *their hands to do wrong. (125.1–3)*

> *When* YHWH *restored the fortunes of Zion,*
> *we were like those who dream.*
> *Then our mouth was filled with laughter,*
> *and our tongue with shouts of joy;*
> *then it was said among the nations,*
> *'*YHWH *has done great things for them.'*
> YHWH *has done great things for us,*
> *and we rejoiced. (126.1–3)*

And both are held within the continuing prayer for protection from enemies:

May all who hate Zion
  be put to shame and turned back.
    (129.5)

All is gathered together in the powerful statement of the establishment of Zion when David brought the Ark of the Covenant back from its exile among the Philistines and planned the building of the shrine in Jerusalem. Psalm 132 retells that story and then announces the divine decree:

For YHWH has chosen Zion;
  he has desired it for his habitation:
'This is my resting-place for ever;
  here I will reside, for I have desired it.
I will abundantly bless its provisions;
  I will satisfy its poor with bread.
Its priests I will clothe with salvation,
  and its faithful will shout for joy.
There I will cause a horn to sprout up for
    David;
  I have prepared a lamp for my anointed one.

His enemies I will clothe with disgrace,
but on him, his crown will gleam.'
(132.13–18)

What vision do we get, what sense of how 'space'
and 'place' work within God's creation and covenant,
when we put all this together? The Psalms not only
insist that we are called to live at the intersection of
God's space and our space, of heaven and earth, to
be (in other words) Temple people. They call us to
live at the intersection of sacred space, the Temple
and the holy land that surrounds it, and the rest of
human space, the world where idolatry and injustice
still wreak their misery.

The Temple turns out to be an advance foretaste
of YHWH's claim on the whole of creation. We are to
see the Temple as establishing, so to speak, a bridgehead for God's own presence within a world that
has very determinedly gone its own way. It is a sign
that the creator God is desiring not to provide a way
to escape from the world (though it may sometimes
feel like that) but to recreate the world from within,
to set up a place within his creation where his
glory will be revealed and his powerful judgments
unveiled.

That is why, as many studies have shown, the Temple was built as a *microcosmos* – a little world. Its design and decoration picked up motifs from Genesis 1 and 2. Those opening chapters of the Bible were in any case all about the creator making a temple, a heaven-and-earth reality, for himself to dwell in, with his image-bearing creatures at its heart.

When, after the six 'days' of creation, the creator completed his work and 'rested', we are to understand not simply that he sat back and did nothing but that he came and took up residence in the world he had made. That is why Psalm 132 speaks twice of the Temple as his 'resting-place' (vv. 8, 14). It is the advance sign of the new creation God longs to bring about.

All other 'meaning' that the Temple then has flows outwards from this point. Think of Psalm 24: having declared that the earth and its fullness belong to YHWH, the psalm then invites us to think of the holiness required to enter his Temple and then to celebrate his own arrival to take up residence there. Israel can then appeal to him: he is in the midst of the city, so it won't be moved; but he will not only protect Zion – he will bring peace to the whole world and be exalted over the nations (Ps. 46).

Again and again the theme comes; it makes no sense, of course, in post-Enlightenment thought, but it fits perfectly within the creational and covenantal monotheism of ancient Israel. 'May YHWH, maker of heaven and earth, bless you from Zion' (134.3).

Just a strange ancient fantasy? So it must appear to many people today – as, no doubt, it did to many people in Jesus's day. By his time, Jerusalem had been overrun this way and that, destroyed and re-built, desecrated and reconsecrated, captured and reorganized – and the new building itself, the project started by Herod the Great to make the Temple the most beautiful and majestic building in the whole world, was well under way but as yet incomplete. (It was finally finished in the fifties of the first century, leaving it standing for less than twenty years before the Romans burned it down one last time.)

How does all that complicated, messy, and ultim-ately tragic history square with the glorious vision we find in one psalm after another?

The beginning of an answer is found in the fact that the tragic history is itself built into the Psalter. The dark and powerful Psalm 74 looks in horror, but without blinking, at the pagan invaders who

are tearing the Temple to bits, describes it all in
terrible detail, and then simply invokes the power
of YHWH as creator. All one can then do is to pray,
'Remember . . .':

> Your foes have roared within your holy
> place;
> they set up their emblems there.
> At the upper entrance they hacked
> the wooden trellis with axes.
> And then, with hatchets and hammers,
> they smashed all its carved work.
> They set your sanctuary on fire;
> they desecrated the dwelling-place of your
> name,
> bringing it to the ground.
> They said to themselves, 'We will utterly
> subdue them';
> they burned all the meeting-places of
> God in the land. . . .
> Yet God my King is from of old,
> working salvation in the earth.
> You divided the sea by your might;
> you broke the heads of the dragons in the
> waters.

You crushed the heads of Leviathan;
you gave him as food for the creatures of
the wilderness. . . .
Yours is the day, yours also the night;
you established the luminaries and
the sun.
You have fixed all the bounds of the earth;
you made summer and winter.
Remember this, O YHWH, *how the enemy*
scoffs,
and an impious people reviles your
name. (74.4–8, 12–14, 16–18)

The God who is supposed to be looking after his own Temple, in other words, is in fact no local or tribal deity. He is the creator himself. Only there is hope to be found, expressed again in the urgings that he will remember, have regard for the covenant, rise up and plead his own cause, and not forget what the wicked are doing.

It is not difficult to imagine devout Jews, in the centuries before Jesus, singing those psalms and longing for their fulfilment. They tell the story, after all, of YHWH going away from his people and then returning once more.

Psalm 78.56–64 looks back to the terrible moment in 1 Samuel 4 when the Philistines captured the Ark, following the wickedness and rebellion of Israel. But then, declares the poem, YHWH himself woke up and took charge. This was the moment when, having formerly dwelt at Shiloh, the divine presence now moved some way south and came to Jerusalem (78.65–69).

For those who sang the Psalms, through into the time of Jesus, this was no mere distant historic reminiscence. One whole strand of thought and prayer, from the time of the Babylonian exile onwards, concerned the belief that YHWH had abandoned the city and the Temple at the time of the original exile because, according to Ezekiel, of similar wickedness and idolatry within Israel (Ezek. 10).

The great exilic prophecies in Ezekiel and in Isaiah 40—66 had insisted that one day YHWH would come back; but although the Temple had been rebuilt a century or so after its destruction by the Babylonians, there are signs that the people were still waiting for his glory to be revealed in the way that Isaiah had promised – a way that would remind them of the glorious moments when the wilderness tabernacle was constructed and dedicated (Exod. 40) or when Solomon's Temple was built and consecrated (1 Kings 8). Malachi (3.1) promises, long years after the exiles had returned, that YHWH *would* one day return to his Temple, but there was no clear sign that this had actually happened.

Those who continued to sing and pray the Psalms throughout this period must, therefore, have been well used to living, as we saw in the previous chapter, in the tension between the past (when he had surely been there), the future (when he would surely return), and the puzzling present (when one might perhaps sense his presence but not yet in the full promised glory and rescuing power). The Psalms picked up the prophetic theme: the glory of YHWH, said Isaiah, will be revealed, and all flesh will see it together; the watchmen will shout for joy as they see YHWH returning to Zion (Isa. 40.5; 52.8).

Yes, replies the psalmist, 'He will speak peace to his people, to his faithful. . . . Surely his salvation is at hand for those who fear him, *that his glory may dwell in our land*' (85.8–9). And as the pagans ruled over Israel through the long post-exilic centuries, this hope, rooted in the Temple theology, resonated sorrowfully in the face of the actual political reality. He had promised to come back, and they sang and hoped and waited. If the glorious claim of the Psalms seems ridiculous to us, we can be sure it often seemed like a fantasy to them as well.

One of the ways the people of Israel came to terms with this sorrow and puzzle was, in various ways and without clear markers, to reverse the imagery. Instead of thinking of a place to which YHWH might come and be at rest, they sometimes thought of YHWH himself as the 'place' where a worshipper might go to be at rest: Sovereign one, says the 'prayer of Moses' in Psalm 90.1, 'you have been our dwelling-place in all generations.' The next psalm picks up the same point:

> You who live in the shelter of the Most High,
>   who abide in the shadow of the
>   Almighty,
> will say to YHWH, 'My refuge and my
>   fortress;
>   my God, in whom I trust.' . . .
> Because you have made YHWH your refuge,
>   the Most High your dwelling-place,
> no evil shall befall you,
>   no scourge come near your tent.
>   (91.1–2, 9–10)

It is not, then, absolutely necessary to be in Jerusalem to know the presence of YHWH. We do not provide a dwelling place for him; he himself is *our* dwelling place.

Psalm 141, another that speaks of YHWH as a 'refuge' (141.8), sees personal and private prayer as the functional equivalent of being in the Temple – a necessity, of course, for the great majority of Jews even before the destruction of the Temple in AD 70, and for all of them thereafter:

> *I call upon you, O YHWH; come quickly*
> > *to me;*
> > *give ear to my voice when I call to you.*
> *Let my prayer be counted as incense*
> > *before you,*
> > *and the lifting up of my hands as an*
> > *evening sacrifice. (141.1–2)*

This doesn't mean that one would not, in fact, prefer to be in the Temple, if that were possible. As we saw, psalms like 42 and 43 express a longing for that, even though the psalmist can still call out to YHWH from far away. But there are other psalms that pick up the prophetic warnings about casual or

formalistic worship and take those warnings a stage
further: YHWH does not actually want the kind of
worship that goes on in the Temple half as much as
he wants an obedient ear and heart. Thus, the following:

> *Sacrifice and offering you do not desire,*
> *but you have given me an open ear.*
> *Burnt-offering and sin-offering*
> *you have not required.*
> *Then I said, 'Here I am;*
> *in the scroll of the book it is written*
> *of me.*
> *I delight to do your will, O my God;*
> *your law is within my heart.' (40.6–8)*

> *'Not for your sacrifices do I rebuke you;*
> *your burnt-offerings are continually*
> *before me.*
> *I will not accept a bull from your house,*
> *or goats from your folds.*
> *For every wild animal of the forest is mine,*
> *the cattle on a thousand hills.*
> *I know all the birds of the air,*
> *and all that moves in the field is mine.*

If I were hungry, I would not tell you,
　　for the world and all that is in it is mine.
Do I eat the flesh of bulls,
　　or drink the blood of goats?
Offer to God a sacrifice of thanksgiving,
　　and pay your vows to the Most High.
Call on me in the day of trouble;
　　I will deliver you, and you shall glorify
　　　　me.' . . .
'Those who bring thanksgiving as their
　　　　sacrifice honour me;
　　to those who go the right way
　　I will show the salvation of God.'
　　　　(50.8–15, 23)

I will praise the name of God with a song;
　　I will magnify him with thanksgiving.
This will please YHWH *more than an ox*
　　or a bull with horns and hoofs.
　　　　(69.30–31)

All this prepares the way for a different kind of 'space', the 'portable Temple' developed by Jews from the time of the Babylonian exile onwards, and on to the present day.

The apparent gap in the cosmos – in the Jewish cosmos in particular – left by YHWH abandoning the Temple in the sixth century BC was at least partially filled by fresh reflections about Israel's God-given law, the Torah. By prayerful and obedient study of the Torah, the blessings that one might have had through the 'sacred space' of the Temple could be obtained anywhere at all:

Happy are those
  who do not follow the advice of the wicked,
or take the path that sinners tread,
  or sit in the seat of scoffers;
but their delight is in the law of YHWH,
  and on his law they meditate day and
    night.
They are like trees
  planted by streams of water,
which yield their fruit in its season,
  and their leaves do not wither.
In all that they do, they prosper. (1.1–3)

People such as those described here, at the opening of the Psalter, are drawing up the life and presence of YHWH by putting their roots down into his word. Psalm 119 is a glorious extended meditation

on the same theme, with the alphabetical backbone
of the poem (each set of eight verses begins with the
next letter of the Hebrew alphabet, a remarkable
poetic feat in itself) making its own point about the
word of God. The very script in which it is written
can bring God's order to human life.

One might pick almost any stanza as an example,
but a particularly rich one is verses 41–48, each line
starting with the Hebrew letter *waw:*

Let your steadfast love come to me, O YHWH,
 your salvation according to your promise.
Then I shall have an answer for those who
   taunt me,
 for I trust in your word.
Do not take the word of truth utterly out of
   my mouth,
 for my hope is in your ordinances.
I will keep your law continually,
 for ever and ever.
I shall walk at liberty,
 for I have sought your precepts.
I will also speak of your decrees before kings,
 and shall not be put to shame;
I find my delight in your commandments,
 because I love them.

I revere your commandments, which I love,
and I will meditate on your statutes.

This kind of language belongs closely with the emphasis, in Psalm 50 and elsewhere, on the obedience of the heart.

Indeed, as we shall see in the next chapter, we have here a sense not only of the Torah as a new kind of 'sacred space' but of the transformative effect of obedience. Wherever you travel, all this implies, the Torah will be like a moving tabernacle, a place of refuge: 'Your statutes have been my songs', says the next stanza, 'wherever I make my home' (119.54).

So, if the Temple was a microcosm, a small version of the whole world, the same is true of the Torah – or, at least, the Temple and Torah between them point ahead to a new world, God's new 'place', the renewed creation filled with God's glory and purpose as the waters cover the sea.

Thus it is that in one of the best-loved of all psalms – number 19, which C. S. Lewis hailed as the finest poem ever written – we find the Torah in parallel with the sun, suggesting that in God's new world, already launched and waiting for worshippers to inhabit it, the Torah plays the role of the sun itself within the present creation. Once again it is hard not to quote the entire psalm:

The heavens are telling the glory of God;
and the firmament proclaims his
handiwork.
Day to day pours forth speech,
and night to night declares knowledge.
There is no speech, nor are there words;
their voice is not heard;
yet their voice goes out through all the earth,
and their words to the end of the world.
In the heavens he has set a tent for the sun,
which comes out like a bridegroom from his
wedding canopy,
and like a strong man runs its course
with joy.
Its rising is from the end of the heavens,
and its circuit to the end of them;
and nothing is hidden from its heat.
The Torah of YHWH *is perfect,*
reviving the soul;
the decrees of YHWH *are sure,*
making wise the simple;

the precepts of YHWH are right,
    rejoicing the heart;
the commandment of YHWH is clear,
    enlightening the eyes;
the fear of YHWH is pure,
    enduring for ever;
the ordinances of YHWH are true
    and righteous altogether.
More to be desired are they than gold,
    even much fine gold;
sweeter also than honey,
    and drippings of the honeycomb.
Moreover by them is your servant warned;
    in keeping them there is great reward.
But who can detect their errors?
    Clear me from hidden faults.
Keep back your servant also from the
       insolent;
    do not let them have dominion over me.
Then I shall be blameless,
    and innocent of great transgression.
Let the words of my mouth and the
       meditation of my heart
    be acceptable to you,
    O YHWH, my rock and my redeemer.

Notice what has happened. The psalms themselves, even while continuing to celebrate the Zion promises and the coming Davidic kingship that goes with them, already sing about, and by singing help to *bring* about, an implicit *personal* version of Temple theology. Devout worshippers, individually or corporately, can themselves become, as it were, an extension of sacred space.

The notion of YHWH dwelling in the Temple has not been abandoned, but it is translated into the notion of his dwelling with his people – *within* his people, wherever they are – through their study and heartfelt practice of the Torah. Through that same Torah, his people discover not only that he can be their 'refuge', the 'place' where they are at home, but that he will make his home with them, within them.

This will, of course, require – and effect! – a radical transformation. If the Temple theology is being democratized and personalized in this fashion, it loses none of its demand for holiness in the process – rather, the reverse.

The psalms are here pointing to the double intention of the creator: that the Temple in Jerusalem should be a sign not only of God's purpose to flood the whole of creation with his glorious presence, but also of his longing to fill the hearts, minds, imaginations and wills of his people with that same glory.

That takes us straight to the subject of the next chapter. But before we get there, we should notice the way in which this sense of sacred space, moving from Temple to Torah to the individual worshipper, finds spectacular fulfilment in the New Testament.

The hope for YHWH's glorious return, which echoes through the Psalms and the prophets, is picked up in various ways by the early Christian writers who believed that it had been fulfilled both in Jesus and in the gift of the Spirit. Near the heart of the early Christian understanding of who Jesus was and is we find the reinhabiting – I use the word advisedly – of the ancient psalmic vision of God dwelling in the Temple.

This is how, it seems, we are to understand the shocking claim, as some translations put it, that 'God was in Christ' (2 Cor. 5.19, KJV). Mark introduces Jesus by pointing to John the Baptist as the 'voice' that, in Isaiah 40, is preparing the way for YHWH's glory to return at last. In case we miss the point, he also aligns him with the 'messenger' who will prepare the people for YHWH himself to come back to his Temple (Mark 1.2–3, quoting Isa. 40.3 and Mal. 3.1).

John introduces Jesus by retelling the story of creation ('In the beginning . . .') and climaxing with a vision of Jesus *as* the new Temple. It is hard to bring out the full flavour of John 1.14 ('The word became flesh, and lived among us'); the Greek word John uses could be translated to say that he 'tabernacles' in our midst. Most translations, naturally, do not put it quite like that, but that is what the word means.

'In him [Jesus]', writes Paul in Colossians 2, 'all the full measure of divinity has taken up bodily residence' (Col. 2.9, compare 1.19); again, this is Temple language. The early Christians, wanting to explain their explosive sense of who Jesus really was, drew on the ancient theme of Israel's God coming back at last to dwell in the midst of his people, to save them and bring his restorative and healing justice to the whole world.

Several other themes join up at this point. The royal theme I mentioned earlier is closely bound up with the Zion traditions; both these themes then come to fresh fulfilment in Jesus who is David's son and hence God's son – not only the Temple *builder*, but the Temple in person.

Suddenly those great Temple psalms burst into fresh flower: On the holy mount stands the city he founded; glorious things are spoken of you, O city of God. How lovely is your dwelling place, YHWH of hosts; one day in your courts is better than a thousand elsewhere. Here is the challenge for those who take the New Testament seriously: try singing those psalms Christologically, thinking of Jesus as their ultimate fulfilment. See how they sound, what they do, where they take you.

But sing them also pneumatologically – that is, reflect, as you sing, on the New Testament's vision of the church as the new Temple, indwelt by the Spirit of the living God. Watch how, without any complex theological or hermeneutical footwork, the early Christian vision of covenant renewal generates a fresh idea of sacred space. Or go back to Psalm 72 and see how those worldwide promises about David's coming kingdom are fulfilled in the New Testament (as, for instance, in Matt. 28.16–20 or Rom. 15.7–13), up to and including the stunning concluding line: 'Blessed be his glorious name for ever; may his glory fill the whole earth. Amen and Amen' (v. 19).

God's glory is, of course, already known in creation, as Psalm 19 so splendidly declares. But there

will be a new filling, a further drenching of the creation with God's presence and glory, so that what was
true of the tabernacle and Temple will ultimately be
true of all creation (Isa. 11; Hab. 2).

The Psalms stand at the intersection of both time
and space, of the present Jerusalem Temple and the
future cosmic Temple. That is close to what Paul is
saying in Romans 8.18–27; it is at the heart of what
John the Visionary is saying when he sketches his
vision of the New Jerusalem in the form of a gigantic
Holy of Holies (Rev. 21), where, as at the end of Ezekiel, the city will be known by the fact that 'YHWH is
There' (Ezek. 48.35).

The New Testament picks up all of these themes,
so central to the Psalter, and sings them in a new key.

There is, of course, still a definite future focus
to it all. The early Christians did not imagine for
a moment that they had 'arrived' at the ultimate
new creation. But with the resurrection of Jesus and
the gift of the Spirit, that new creation had already
broken into the world, and they were able to sing the
ancient songs with, as it were, a whole new set of har-
monies. Learning to sing them that way formed the
heart of early Christian spirituality and the taproot
of early Christian mission.

This did not mean that the early Christians were able to leave behind the Psalms of lament. Jesus himself had prayed Psalm 22 as he hung on the cross, and the early Christians found themselves following him and (as he had warned) carrying their own crosses in turn. They had to learn to understand their own often painful and frightening situation according to the pattern Jesus had established.

If the Psalms provide a sense of sacred space, that space is where celebration and sorrow are held together within the powerful love and presence of the one God. We see in the Psalms themselves that the claim they celebrate – the belief that the living God has made his home in Jerusalem – comes at a huge cost: enemies attacking from outside, corruption threatening from within.

The early Christians, making exactly the same claim about Jesus and his death (that in him, and in these events, the living God had returned to Jerusalem at last to judge and to save), saw that huge cost finally being borne. They were then able to translate it once more, out into the wider world in which they themselves, as followers of the crucified Messiah, faced persecution and danger.

Thus, if Jesus had taken the complaints and laments of Psalms 22 and 69 and made them his own, Paul in turn picked up similar complaints from elsewhere in the Psalter. In one of his most famous passages, he quotes Psalm 44: 'Because of you', he writes, 'we are being killed all day long; / We are regarded as sheep destined for slaughter' (Ps. 44.22, quoted by Paul in Rom. 8.36). This, it seems, is part of what he means by being 'shaped according to the model of the image of his son' (Rom. 8.29).

Indeed, that quotation is not the first hint of Psalm 44 in the passage in question. In Romans 8.27 Paul speaks of God as 'the Searcher of Hearts' and who therefore knows what the Spirit is thinking and saying, even though the worshipper is only conscious of inarticulate groanings. But this mention of God as the heart searcher is also taken from Psalm 44, in the verse (21) immediately before the one Paul quotes a bit later: God knows, says the psalmist, 'the secrets of the heart'. The whole psalm, in fact, resonates with the whole of Romans 8, though it would take us too far afield at present to explore this in detail.

The underlying point is this: the Temple theology that is so characteristic of the Psalms had already developed in the direction of a Torah theology, in which the devout worshipper could be assured of God's presence and love in any geographical location; and this in turn gave birth to a sense that the living God would come to dwell not just within the Temple but within the worshippers themselves. Paul speaks in Romans 8.9–11 of the 'indwelling' of the Spirit, and then in 8.12–17 of the 'leading' of the Spirit, in ways that echo the ancient biblical language about Israel's God 'dwelling' in the tabernacle in the wilderness and leading the Israelites to the promised land. Paul speaks in 8.1–8 of the Spirit achieving 'what the Torah . . . was incapable of doing', giving at last the 'life' that the Torah promised but that the unredeemed sinfulness of humankind, Israel included, could not attain. All of this is accomplished through the rescuing and restorative action of the Messiah himself, coming into his 'inheritance' – the whole renewed world! – just as Psalm 2 had promised (Rom. 8.17).

We should not be surprised, then, that Paul finds in the Psalms both a map to see where he is at present (rejoicing in God's victory while still surrounded by persecution and danger of every kind) and a means by which he can bring both his celebrations and his sorrows into the personal presence of the God who searches the hearts.

The psalmists' notions of sacred space have not been abandoned. They have been translated into the mode of Messiah and Spirit. The 'sacred space' of the Temple, the primary location for so many psalms, stood at the heart of God's holy land. Paul has glimpsed a vision in which the whole world is now God's holy land and is to be set free at last from its slavery to corruption, flooded at last (as the prophets had said) with the knowledge and glory of God.

And at the heart of that new land, we see not a sacred building of bricks and mortar but a sacred *people*, whose very hearts have become the dwelling place of the living God by his Spirit, enabling them to be conformed to 'the model of the image of his son', the one in whom the Psalms' greatest promises have found their fulfilment. The psalmists' multi-layered vision of sacred space has become a reality and is to become so yet more fully, through the very things that the psalmists themselves promised: the coming of the Messiah and the transformation of human hearts and lives by the personal presence of God himself.

Chapter 5

All the Trees of the
Forest Sing for Joy

THE PSALMS CELEBRATE THE TRANSFORMATION of time; they stand at the intersection of space – God's space and ours – and they do something very similar with what we may call 'matter'. The Psalms celebrate – in fact, they positively relish – the sheer physicality of creation: its stuff and substance, its seed-times and harvests, the winds and the rocks, the nights and the days. 'Matter' may not be the best word to use for all of this, but our modern trio of time, space and matter enable us to get the picture and now to focus attention on the third of them.

This one is, if anything, harder for us than the first two. I spoke earlier about the mind-set of

Western modernity. We have been heavily influenced on the one hand by Epicureanism, in which God or 'the gods' are separated from the world we know by a great and unbridgeable gulf. And we have been shaped on the other hand by a residual Platonism, in which the material world is a shabby, corrupt place to be endured while we have to and escaped when we can.

That is a fairly devastating combination, which has led many Christians to imagine that 'this world is not my home; I'm just a-passing through'. People quote Jesus's saying to Pilate – in the words of the King James Version – that his kingdom was 'not of this world' (John 18.36), as though Jesus was endorsing that Platonic vision of leaving the present world altogether and going off to a different one, a world (perhaps) of pure spirit, not only away from the 'material' world but outside time and space as we know it.

What Jesus said and meant was in fact that his kingdom was not *from* this world. The kingdoms that grow up from within the world make their way by fighting, but Jesus's kingdom proceeds on a different basis. His kingdom was and is most emphatically *for* this world. I have written about these things elsewhere. (See *Surprised by Hope* (SPCK, 2011) and *How God*

Became King (SPCK, 2012).) But the wrong impression remains in many hearts and minds.

Our modern Western worldviews have made it seriously difficult for us to hear Psalm 19.1–2 as anything but a pretty fantasy. We looked at it in the previous chapter, but it bears repetition:

> *The heavens are telling the glory of God;*
> *and the firmament proclaims his*
> *handiwork.*
> *Day to day pours forth speech,*
> *and night to night declares knowledge.*

To think of this as mere dreaming, a kind of poetic licence, is to miss the point, which is that all creation does in fact praise its maker.

Our problem is that we have allowed the ears of our hearts to be closed to what is in fact going on. When our own poets try to draw our attention to it – I think of Thomas Traherne, for instance, or William Blake – we find them a bit strange as well.

But the vision of creation praising its maker is, after all, there in the New Testament as well – indeed, in one of the New Testament's greatest visions. In the heavenly throne room glimpsed by John the Visionary, the 'four living creatures' praise God without stopping, day and night, singing,

> *Holy, holy, holy,*
> *Lord God Almighty,*
>> *Who Was and Who Is and Who Is*
>> *to Come. (Rev. 4.8)*

The humans in the scene then join in the song and add other dimensions. But my present point is this: what looks to the flattened-out imagination of late Western modernity like 'lifeless' matter is in fact a world throbbing with God-given life. That life is constantly praising its maker by being, particularly and peculiarly, what it is.

Only humans, it seems, have the capacity to live as something other than what they are (God reflectors, image bearers). Trees behave as trees; rocks as rocks; the sea is and does what the sea is and does. And the psalmists look out on it all and see it as a great shout of praise to the God who has made it to be and to flourish:

> *By your strength you established the*
>> *mountains;*

> *you are girded with might. . . .*
> *Those who live at earth's farthest bounds are*
>   *awed by your signs;*
> *you make the gateways of the morning and*
>   *the evening shout for joy. (65.6, 8)*

That last line means, I think, that the psalmist saw, as we mostly do, something special and evocative in the quality of light at either end of the day. But he heard, as we mostly do not, something else going on: a shout of joy at this moment of strange, transient glory. And the joy is increased as, with every passing harvest, what we have come to see as 'the natural order' is understood as the work of God himself, making the earth fertile and fruitful:

> *You visit the earth and water it,*
>   *you greatly enrich it;*
> *the river of God is full of water;*
>   *you provide the people with grain,*
>   *for so you have prepared it.*
> *You water its furrows abundantly,*
>   *settling its ridges,*
> *softening it with showers,*
>   *and blessing its growth.*
> *You crown the year with your bounty;*

> *your wagon tracks overflow with*
> *richness.*
> *The pastures of the wilderness overflow,*
> *the hills gird themselves with joy,*
> *the meadows clothe themselves with flocks,*
> *the valleys deck themselves with grain,*
> *they shout and sing together for joy.*
> *(65.9–13)*

The whole countryside, in fact, is putting on its fine clothes as if getting ready for a party: God's party, the harvest season that humans facilitate but do not create. (It is an indication of how far contemporary Western society has cut itself off from the agricultural roots, to which all societies before our own have been close, that we have to blink and rub our eyes to see the fields and the hillsides in this way.)

I have learned, in my advancing years, to take all this more seriously than a normal Western worldview would suggest. The old Anglican prayer book prescribes, to be prayed daily, Psalm 95 with its celebration of God's creative power:

> *For* YHWH *is a great God,*
> *and a great King above all gods.*
> *In his hand are the depths of the earth;*

the heights of the mountains are his also.
The sea is his, for he made it,
  and the dry land, which his hands have
    formed. (95.3–5)

The service of morning prayer then moves on, after the reading from the Old Testament, to the ancient hymn called 'Te Deum', which begins in similar fashion:

We praise thee, O God,
  we acknowledge thee to be the Lord;
all the earth doth worship thee,
  the Father everlasting.

All the earth! Well, the seraphim in Isaiah's vision declared that the whole earth was full of YHWH's glory (Isa. 6.3). With that to one side of us and the answering hymn in Revelation 4 to the other, why should we not look out on the fruitful earth around us, whether it be mountains and lakes or simply a plant on a windowsill, and celebrate the fact that it is all singing praise to its maker? That, indeed, is part of what it means when we say in the Creed that we believe in 'God the Father almighty, *Maker of heaven and earth*'. Unless our worship is joined – more or less consciously – with the praises of all creation, there should be a question mark as to whether it really is genuine Christian worship.

This brings us back to a point we noticed before: in various passages in the Old Testament, we are told that God's glory either *already* fills the whole earth, as in the angelic hymn of Isaiah 6, or that it will do so one day.

Psalm 72 expresses this as clearly as anywhere else. It begins with the king being endowed by God with the ability to do justice among the people, summoning the natural landscape to contribute as well:

> *May he judge your people with*
> *righteousness,*
> *and your poor with justice.*
> *May the mountains yield prosperity for the*
> *people,*
> *and the hills, in righteousness.*
> *May he defend the cause of the poor of the*
> *people,*
> *give deliverance to the needy,*
> *and crush the oppressor.* (72.2–4)

The central blessings of creation itself will then function both as a simile for the way in which the rule of the true king will bring justice and peace to the world, and also as a marker of time, praying that this righteous rule will last as long as do the sun and moon themselves:

> *May he live while the sun endures,*
> > *and as long as the moon, throughout all*
> > > *generations.*
> *May he be like rain that falls on the mown*
> > *grass,*
> > *like showers that water the earth.*
> *In his days may righteousness flourish*
> > *and peace abound, until the moon is no*
> > > *more. (72.5–7)*

There then follows the prayer for the worldwide rule of the coming king, which is to be welcomed on the basis that he will deliver the needy, rescue the poor, and have pity on the weak and helpless (72.8–14). This leads into a prayer that combines the blessings of royal rule with the blessings of creation, taking the poem naturally, and not simply as an afterthought, into the prayer for the divine glory to fill the whole world.

Reading the passage in reverse order, in fact, we see what this idea of the earth being filled with divine glory actually means: it means on the one hand the glorious combination of creation being fully alive, fully itself, and on the other hand human society being properly ordered through justice and prosperity.

> *Long may he live!*
> *May gold of Sheba be given to him.*
> *May prayer be made for him continually,*
>   *and blessings invoked for him all day*
>   *long.*
> *May there be abundance of grain in the*
>   *land;*
>   *may it wave on the tops of the*
>   *mountains;*
>   *may its fruit be like Lebanon;*
> *and may people blossom in the cities*
>   *like the grass of the field.*
> *May his name endure for ever,*
>   *his fame continue as long as the sun.*
> *May all nations be blessed in him;*
>   *may they pronounce him happy.*
> *Blessed be* YHWH, *the God of Israel,*
>   *who alone does wondrous things.*

Blessed be his glorious name for ever;
may his glory fill the whole earth. Amen
and Amen. (72.15–19)

The ultimate goal, of the whole earth being filled with God's glory, is spoken of elsewhere in the Old Testament. (See Num. 14.21, Hab. 2.14, and compare Isa. 11.9, where the earth is filled with the *knowledge* of YHWH, at the end of a passage about the righteous rule of the coming king, quite similar in its way to Ps. 72.) This, as we saw in the previous chapter, is basically Temple theology.

What some had experienced, or might hope to experience, in the tabernacle or Temple (the tent or house being filled with the glory of YHWH) was now to be hoped for in terms of the whole creation. That, we may assume, is part at least of what Jesus taught his followers to pray for when they were to say, 'Thy kingdom come, *on earth as in heaven.*'

But if this is the ultimate goal, there are steps on the road toward it – steps by which the material world can be seen as already taken up within that divine purpose, not simply waiting in a state of sorry decay for something new to happen.

These stages on the way are already marked in those great psalms of creation, 103 and 104. Psalm 103 praises God for all the blessings of human life and especially for the compassion and gentleness with which God treats his frail and weak human children. All of human life is set within the larger vision of God's kingdom, his sovereignty over heaven and earth (103.19), and the psalmist can therefore summon all of God's works to praise him, wherever they are 'in all places of his dominion' (103.22).

This is then translated into a different mode in Psalm 104. First, instead of describing what God has done and is doing, and summoning his creation to praise him, Psalm 104 speaks to God himself, so that the word 'you' occurs twenty or more times:

> O YHWH *my God, you are very great.*
> *You are clothed with honour and majesty. . . .*
> *You stretch out the heavens like a tent,*
> > *you set the beams of your chambers on*
> > > *the waters,*
> *you make the clouds your chariot,*
> > *you ride on the wings of the wind,*
> *you make the winds your messengers,*
> > *fire and flame your ministers.*

You set the earth on its foundations,
so that it shall never be shaken.
You cover it with the deep as with a
garment . . . (104.1–6)

And so on and so on, celebrating the mountains and hills, the streams and valleys, the animals and birds that live on what grows and flows (as we say) 'by itself' but, in fact, as the objects of God's care and provision:

By the streams the birds of the air have their
habitation;
they sing among the branches.
From your lofty abode you water the
mountains;
the earth is satisfied with the fruit of your
work. (104.12–13)

Humans are at last allowed on the scene, making their appearance, as in Genesis 1, when the stage has been fully set:

You cause the grass to grow for the cattle,
and plants for people to use,
to bring forth food from the earth,

> *and wine to gladden the human heart,*
> *oil to make the face shine,*
> *and bread to strengthen the human*
> *heart. (104.14–15)*

Then comes the moment, at the heart of the psalm, that I regard as one of the great lines in all of scripture, a moment that draws together Genesis and Proverbs and looks on to the poetry of St Paul. God has created the world in such a way that the great lights of the sky – the sun and the moon – bring order to the life of animals and humans alike. Observing this, the psalmist celebrates the amazing multiplicity of God's creation and the fact that it is done 'in wisdom', wisely:

> *You have made the moon to mark the*
> *seasons;*
> *the sun knows its time for setting.*
> *You make darkness, and it is night,*
> *when all the animals of the forest come*
> *creeping out.*
> *The young lions roar for their prey,*
> *seeking their food from God.*
> *When the sun rises, they withdraw*
> *and lie down in their dens.*

People go out to their work
  and to their labour until the evening.
O YHWH, *how manifold are your works!*
  In wisdom you have made them all;
  the earth is full of your creatures.
    (104.19–24)

'In wisdom': the Hebrew is *behokmah*. Proverbs 8.22 says that 'YHWH created me at the beginning of his work'; and this, in turn, looks back to *berēshith*, 'in the beginning', the first word of scripture.

This is the line of thought that Paul picks up in the glorious poem of Colossians 1.15–20, in which he sets out, after the fashion indeed of a Hebrew psalm, the balanced account of all things being *created* in, through, and for the Messiah and then all things being *redeemed* in, through and for him. Paul leaves us in no doubt that he is picking up this tradition of 'creation through wisdom', joining together Genesis 1 and Proverbs 8. The Messiah, he says, 'is the place where you'll find all the hidden treasures of wisdom and knowledge' (Col. 2.2–3); and *he is the beginning, the firstborn from the dead* – he, through whom all things were made:

He is the image of God, the invisible one,
The firstborn of all creation.

For in him all things were created,
In the heavens and here on the earth.
Things we can see and things we cannot –
Thrones and lordships and rulers and
          powers –
All things were created both through him
          and for him.
And he is ahead, prior to all else,
And in him all things hold together;
And he himself is supreme, the head
Over the body, the church.
He is the start of it all,
Firstborn from realms of the dead;
So in all things he might be the chief.
For in him all the Fullness was glad to dwell
And through him to reconcile all to himself,
Making peace through the blood of his cross,
Through him – yes, things on the earth,
And also the things in the heavens.
          (Col. 1.15–20)

Everything that Israel's scriptures had said about
'beginning' and 'wisdom' has come rushing together
in Jesus himself. The resurrection has gloriously
reaffirmed the goodness and God-givenness of the

creation (over against any suggestion of Platonic dualism) and has restated God's intention to fill it all to overflowing with his own love and life and glory. Thus, although creation as it now stands must go through the valley of the shadow of death, God will bring it to new life by his Spirit, and this will lead to the great prayer that the glory of YHWH may last for ever, that YHWH may rejoice in his works.

'Matter' matters because it is God's 'matter', made not as a temporary ornament for a world doomed to decay and death but as the raw material for the new world full of glory.

These all look to you
  to give them their food in due season;
when you give to them, they gather it up;
  when you open your hand, they are filled
    with good things.
When you hide your face, they are
    dismayed;
  when you take away their breath,
    they die
  and return to their dust.
When you send forth your spirit, they are
    created;

and you renew the face of the ground.
May the glory of YHWH *endure for ever;*
  may YHWH *rejoice in his works –*
who looks on the earth and it trembles,
  who touches the mountains and they
    smoke.
I will sing to YHWH *as long as I live;*
  I will sing praise to my God while I have
    being.
May my meditation be pleasing to him,
  for I rejoice in YHWH. *(104.27–34)*

When we put this together with the testimony of the
New Testament – which is not difficult – then we
find a remarkable vista before us. The 'wisdom' by
which the one true God made the world and all its
creatures is to be identified with and as the one we
now know in and as Jesus the Messiah.

This is the God who placed his glory in the Jerusalem Temple but who now wants his glory to last
for ever in the creation that, renewed by the spirit,
will be freed from all evil (v. 35) and become the
wonderful vessel of that same glory.

Once we learn to understand the overlap of time
in the Psalms (past and future both colouring the

present), once we learn to understand the overlap of space in the Psalms (God's glory now in the Temple, now in the Torah, now in the whole of creation), it is not too great a stretch to see that 'matter' itself, the material world, is designed to be flooded with God's glory. And if this is so for the whole creation – trees and seas and birds and animals – it is so above all for human beings.

The mode in which that glory is to be seen in the present is praise. 'I will sing praise to my God while I have being.' The glory of God, said the theologian Irenaeus, is a human being fully alive. The writer of Psalm 104, and we may hope the singer as well, is one such human being, not only celebrating God's filling of the earth with his glory but embodying that same reality in the life of praise.

Why, after all, would a good God make a world that is other than himself? God does not, as some of the rabbis proposed (and as some modern theologians have argued), *retreat* from filling all things in order that there may be room for things other than himself. That implies a very different God from the one we see in the Psalms, not to mention the New Testament.

God creates 'that which is not God' *out of gener-ous love* in order that he may then in the end fill it, flood it, drench it, with his love and his glory.

Here is the paradox at the heart of the ancient biblical vision of creation, a paradox that reaches its height in the person of Jesus himself and then in the lives of all who are indwelt by his Spirit. God creates us to be precisely *other than God* because that is what love – the divine love – is like. God has taken great delight in the whale and the anteater, in the cedar tree and the rosebush, in the wild asses and the slimy, creeping things of the sea, in the lions roaring for their food and the little furry animals scurrying around the mountain rocks. All that is already there in Psalm 104 and elsewhere. This is the sheer matter of the world.

So, as with time and space, we are invited to stand at the intersection of original created matter and the matter of new creation, the original matter that reveals God's power and glory and the new creation that will be flooded, saturated with God's presence and glory. And we do not, of course, stand there as mere outside observers. We, being ourselves part of that extraordinary picture, find our own stories within the larger narrative of creation – our own small but significant stories of wine and bread, of work and rest, of death and new life and, through it all, of praise.

Psalm 104, of course, does not stand alone – even though it is, in its way, beyond comparison. Its themes are taken up elsewhere: for instance, in Psalm 145, where YHWH provides food for every living thing and watches over them with his love, so that the psalmist can summon all creatures to join in his praise. Many other passages echo the same set of themes.

Sometimes this combination of celebration and praise bursts out in more dramatic mode, as in Psalm 29:

> *Ascribe to* YHWH, *O heavenly beings,*
> *ascribe to* YHWH *glory and strength.*
> *Ascribe to* YHWH *the glory of his name;*
> *worship* YHWH *in holy splendour. (29.1–2)*

In Psalm 33.6–9, it is the 'word' of YHWH that functioned as his active agent in creating all things. Here in Psalm 29, it is the 'voice' of YHWH that is the living, active force, going out in power, shaking everything up, and (we note in particular) causing those in his temple to speak of his 'glory':

The voice of YHWH *is over the waters;*
    the God of glory thunders,
    YHWH, *over mighty waters.*
The voice of YHWH *is powerful;*
    the voice of YHWH *is full of majesty.*
The voice of YHWH *breaks the cedars;*
    YHWH *breaks the cedars of Lebanon.*
He makes Lebanon skip like a calf,
    and Sirion like a young wild ox.
The voice of YHWH *flashes forth flames*
        of fire.
The voice of YHWH *shakes the wilderness;*
    YHWH *shakes the wilderness of Kadesh.*
The voice of YHWH *causes the oaks to whirl,*
    and strips the forest bare;
    and in his temple all say, 'Glory!'
        (29.3–9)

This can all then be summed up in the vision of God as king and his people gaining strength and peace from his sovereign rule:

YHWH *sits enthroned over the flood;*
    YHWH *sits enthroned as king for ever.*
May YHWH *give strength to his people!*

May YHWH *bless his people with peace!*
(29.10–11)

There is, of course, a constant tension in the
Psalms between the celebration of creation the way
it is and the longing for YHWH to come and put it all
right at last. The reason for this tension, so characteristic of all scriptural thought in one way or another, is
never explored in itself.

The Psalms do not, that is, offer us an answer
to 'the problem of evil'. But they are clear where
the answer is *not* to be found. It is not to be found
where the pantheist wants to find it, suggesting that
'evil' is merely a matter of our perception and that
the world just is the way it is and we should get used
to it.

Nor is it to be found where the dualist wants
to find it, suggesting that the whole of 'matter' (and
time and space as well) is bad, evil, dangerous and
seductive and that we should find ways of escaping it
all in a detached spirituality in the present and in a
distant non-material 'salvation' in the future.

Instead, the psalmists again and again celebrate
the promise that the creator of the world will renew
his creation, 'judging' it in the sense of pronouncing

definitively against all that has corrupted and defaced it, and putting it right once and for all.

As we have already seen, this will involve the setting right of all human wrongs, with particular attention being given to the poor, the weak, and the defenceless. But it will go much wider and deeper, leading to a 'judgment', a 'putting right', for the whole of creation.

We looked at Romans 8 in the last chapter; in the Psalms, particularly some of the psalms between 90 and 100, we find the roots of this idea of creation as a whole being liberated, by the creator himself, so as to be fully itself at last.

Psalm 93 celebrates YHWH as king of the world, able to resist all forces of chaos:

> *The floods have lifted up, O YHWH,*
> > *the floods have lifted up their voice;*
> > *the floods lift up their roaring.*
> *More majestic than the thunders of mighty*
> > *waters,*
> > *more majestic than the waves of the sea,*
> > *majestic on high is YHWH!*
> > *(93.3–4)*

But this only, as it were, states the premise for what is to come. Psalm 94 complains of the arrogance of the wicked and longs for YHWH to sort things out, to give what they deserve to those who kill the widow, the stranger and the orphan, supposing that because there is no human to remonstrate on their behalf that there is no God to do so either (94.5–7). The tone of voice throughout Psalm 94 indicates that the joyful claims about coming cosmic judgment issued in the subsequent poems are not to be made casually. The present state, in which the world still awaits final judgment, is painful and puzzling; Psalm 94 looks back, in this respect, to Psalm 73 in particular. God is the creator (94.8–11); he therefore has the responsibility and the capacity to be the judge, and justice will be done at last (94.15, 23).

The cosmic dramas of Psalms 93 to 99 thus include within themselves the human dramas of actual injustice that produce the longing that the cosmic promises might come true in smaller human situations as well. They also, therefore, include the summons and warning: those who invoke YHWH as the judge of all must themselves live in the light of that coming judgment. That is where the sudden warning of Psalm 95 (sometimes omitted in liturgical use, but always powerfully relevant) comes into its own: remember what happened to the people wandering in the wilderness. It is all very well to praise YHWH and to celebrate his creation, but your own life must then be brought into line, without grumbling or murmuring (95.7–11).

This then opens the way for those great celebrations, the 'new songs' of Psalms 96 and 98. YHWH is the creator and is to be worshipped as such, but he is also the one who will come to put all things right at last:

> *Say among the nations, 'YHWH is king!*
> > *The world is firmly established; it shall*
> > > *never be moved.*
> > *He will judge the peoples with equity.'*
> *Let the heavens be glad, and let the earth*
> > *rejoice;*
> > *let the sea roar, and all that fills it;*
> > *let the field exult, and everything in it.*
> *Then shall all the trees of the forest sing*
> > *for joy*
> > *before YHWH; for he is coming,*
> > *for he is coming to judge the earth.*

He will judge the world with righteousness,
and the peoples with his truth. (96.10–13)

This is why Psalm 97 can then call the whole earth and Zion in particular to celebrate and be glad for what YHWH is doing and will do. 'The heavens proclaim his righteousness,' declares the Psalm, 'and all the peoples behold his glory' (97.6).

Once again we move to a 'new song', perhaps an indication that these songs are looking ahead to the new things that YHWH is going to do, further revelations in action of his character as creator and judge. He has already 'made known his victory', the victory won by his 'right hand and his holy arm', so that all the ends of the earth can see it (98.2, 1, 3, reminding us of Isa. 52.7–12). Now, as his people praise him uninhibitedly and summon all the earth to join in, they are to look to the future and celebrate the fact that he will return at last to put the whole world right:

Let the sea roar, and all that fills it;
the world and those who live in it.
Let the floods clap their hands;
let the hills sing together for joy

> *at the presence of* YHWH, *for he is coming*
> *to judge the earth.*
> *He will judge the world with righteousness,*
> *and the peoples with equity. (98.7–9)*

Here are poems to encourage and inspire those who work in the present for the renewal of creation, for its healing and restoration. And the sequence closes, appropriately enough, with a further celebration of YHWH as king (99.1–5), leading to a meditation on the way YHWH treated his people of old – Moses, Aaron, and Samuel in particular – and a summons to the holiness that must characterize the people who invoke this king, this kingdom, this coming judge (99.5, 9; see also 93.5 and, of course, frequently elsewhere).

The seas and floods, the fields and the animals are celebrating because YHWH is coming to judge. *Time:* the past of creation, the future of judgment, and the present of celebration are drawn together. *Space:* what was promised for the Temple is now promised for the whole world. And now *matter:* we find ourselves standing at the fault line between the original material of creation and the new, restored, glory-filled material of the world that is to be.

This, as I have suggested elsewhere, is the world-view with which we must approach the whole of scripture, not least the Gospels, if we want to understand them instead of dismissing them because they break the mould of our Epicurean or Platonic expectations. (See *Simply Jesus*, ch. 11.)

The same themes come bursting through again as the Psalter accelerates through the 140s to its final climax, like a symphony speeding up toward its glorious conclusion. YHWH is gracious and merciful, slow to anger and abounding in steadfast love. This is who he is not just for some people some of the time but for the whole creation – though the people who know YHWH for themselves will have a special responsibility to make his name known in all the world, a mandate that the early Christian missionaries saw themselves as fulfilling:

> YHWH *is good to all,*
> *and his compassion is over all that he*
> *has made.*
> *All your works shall give thanks to you,*
> O YHWH,
> *and all your faithful shall bless you.*

They shall speak of the glory of your kingdom,
*   and tell of your power,*
to make known to all people your mighty
*   deeds,*
*   and the glorious splendour of your*
*   kingdom.*
Your kingdom is an everlasting kingdom,
*   and your dominion endures throughout*
*   all generations. (145.9–13)*

Once again, this is illustrated by YHWH's provision of food for every living thing (145.15–16). What we with our Deist or Epicurean worldview might call 'instinct' – animals hunting for food – the psalmist sees as the divine activity, ceaselessly providing for the world:

Sing to YHWH with thanksgiving;
*   make melody to our God on the lyre.*
He covers the heavens with clouds,
*   prepares rain for the earth,*
*   makes grass grow on the hills.*
He gives to the animals their food,
*   and to the young ravens when they cry.*
*   (147.7–9)*

God feeds the animals, then, and is kind to those who call upon him. God may be building up Jerusalem (147.2, 13), but he is also out there in the wild, making grass grow on the hills and feeding the young ravens when they call to him. Equally, in 147.15–19, we find a picture somewhat like a wintry version of Psalm 19. There, it was the powerful sun that functioned as an image of the Torah, penetrating into every part of the personality; this time, it is the snow:

> *He sends out his command to the earth;*
> *   his word runs swiftly.*
> *He gives snow like wool;*
> *   he scatters frost like ashes.*
> *He hurls down hail like crumbs –*
> *   who can stand before his cold?*
> *He sends out his word, and melts them;*
> *   he makes his wind blow, and the waters*
> *   flow.*
> *He declares his word to Jacob,*
> *   his statutes and ordinances to Israel.*
> *   (147.15–19)*

All of creation is summoned to worship. Psalm 148 is like a smaller version of the 'Song of the

Three', the great hymn that Shadrach, Meshach and Abednego sang in the burning fiery furnace (this is found in the Apocrypha of the Old Testament, as an addition to the book of Daniel). That, indeed, is part of the point: the three heroes had been commanded to worship the golden image that Nebuchadnezzar had set up, and being loyal Jews, committed to worshipping only the one creator God, they refused. But when people reject pagan idolatry, it is all too easy for them to hide in a kind of dualism, fearing the material world in case it turns out to be a place of demons.

The more appropriate reaction is to summon the whole creation, bit by bit, to praise its maker: 'Bless the Lord, all you works of the Lord,' they sang, proceeding from angels and other higher powers through the elements of creation – the sun, moon and stars, and everything else. Finally, they placed themselves within the summons, using their original Hebrew names: 'Bless the Lord, Hananiah, Azariah, and Mishael; sing praise to him and highly exalt him for ever' (Song of the Three, 66). The fire cannot harm them. God's victory over the powers of evil is accomplished not by running away from the world but by calling the world, the whole creation, to worship.

That is the effect of Psalm 148:

Praise YHWH!
Praise YHWH *from the heavens;*
 praise him in the heights!
Praise him, all his angels;
 praise him, all his host!
Praise him, sun and moon;
 praise him, all you shining stars!
Praise him, you highest heavens,
 and you waters above the heavens!
Let them praise the name of YHWH,
 for he commanded and they were
 created.
He established them for ever and ever;
 he fixed their bounds, which cannot be
 passed.
Praise YHWH *from the earth,*
 you sea monsters and all deeps,
fire and hail, snow and frost,
 stormy wind fulfilling his command!
Mountains and all hills,
 fruit trees and all cedars!
Wild animals and all cattle,
 creeping things and flying birds!

Kings of the earth and all peoples,
    princes and all rulers of the earth!
Young men and women alike,
    old and young together!
Let them praise the name of YHWH,
    for his name alone is exalted;
        his glory is above earth and heaven.
He has raised up a horn for his people,
    praise for all his faithful,
        for the people of Israel who are close
            to him.
Praise YHWH!

This mention of 'kings of the earth' (v. 11) sends us forward to Psalm 149, where part of the reason for celebration and praise is the victory of God over the kings and nobles who have oppressed the peoples of the world (149.7–9). This penultimate psalm thus forms a large circle with Psalm 2, right back at the start of the collection, in which the coming king, hailed by YHWH as 'my son', will be given the nations as his inheritance and will turn their threats and scoffing into respect and obedience.

To put it in modern shorthand, you find the political message *within* the 'creational' message. Once you summon the whole of creation to praise its maker, you can begin to see clearly where the fault lines lie within the world of human power.

Our attempts at political theology lurch to and fro between the political equivalents of pantheism (assuming that things must be left to go on under their own steam by the automatic operation of due process) and dualism (assuming that things are so bad that the only solution is either to opt out and retreat into a private sphere or to revolt and change the system entirely).

The Psalms offer a different vision: a people of praise who, out of their celebration of God's goodness in creation and out of their eager anticipation of his coming in judgment at last, speak his word and his truth to those in power, reminding them that they are answerable to the God who will one day hold them accountable.

And so we come at last to Psalm 150, in which 'everything that breathes' is summoned to praise YHWH for all they are worth. It was, after all, his breath in the first place – his to give, his to take back, and his to give again (as in 104.29–30).

But its main purpose was and is his praise. And again we must stress this point: in the Psalms, the creatures that give God praise are the *physical, material* creatures. Their bodies are not irrelevant physical cupboards in which the truly 'spiritual' parts are stored.

Matter matters; it matters so much that God becomes human and in the resurrection launches that transformed matter, that immortal physicality, to which (I have been suggesting) the Psalms already point forward.

The Psalms offer us a powerful vision in the form of a celebration of God as creator and God as judge; and when, in the last centuries before Jesus and the first centuries after him, first the Jews and then the Christians eagerly explored the promise of resurrection itself, they all saw – both Jews and Christians – that 'resurrection' is what you get once you embrace those two other doctrines: the good creation and the promise that the same creator God will one day sort it all out.

The material world matters; our human material bodies matter because the God who made them will remake them, and what we do with them in the present, as Paul insists to the Corinthians, is a genuine anticipation of what they will be in the future (1 Cor. 6.14).

It shouldn't be difficult, then, to make the transposition at this point into the early Christian vision of Jesus and the Spirit and the way in which the material world is both celebrated and renewed through their work.

The Jewish basis for the early Christian patterns of belief and behaviour is clear. It is important that God's people are embodied, because God made this world and has no intention of abandoning it. The material of creation is a vessel made to be filled with God's new life and glory, even though the transformation may involve suffering, persecution and martyrdom.

The psalmist would look on and say, 'I told you so': Do not some of the most gloriously hopeful psalms sit side by side with some of the most desperate and fearful? The victories of Psalms 108 and 110 stand guard, as it were, over the solemn and terrifying Psalm 109. The sorrows of Psalm 22 give way to the calm vision of Psalm 23, and so to the shout of praise of Psalm 24.

The fresh revelation of glory will only be known through the sorrow and shame of God's people and God's king. As in Psalm 126, it is the one who goes on his way weeping, bearing the seed for sowing, who will come again with joy as he brings home his sheaves.

Seed-time and harvest are themselves, in fact, one of the central ways in which we stand at the corner between the matter of the old world, sown in sorrow and fear, and the matter of the new, reaped in triumph and joy. That is the image Paul picks up in 1 Corinthians 15 when he wants to explain the difference between the present body, made of corruptible 'flesh', and the future body, a solid physical body that is nevertheless incorruptible and undecaying because unlike the present body it will be animated by God's own spirit (1 Cor. 15.35–49).

It is an appropriate image, not just a miscellaneous metaphor. Seed-time and harvest, like day and night, are built into the present creation as signposts, indications that the God who made the world has new purposes yet to be unveiled. Jesus himself used the same image to speak of his own forthcoming death and resurrection (John 12.24).

In all of this, we sense the larger world within which the uses of the Psalms in the New Testament make the sense they do. *Jesus, the human, bodily son of Mary, has become the place where and the means by which the glory of the Lord has been revealed for all flesh to see it together.*

And as we see the glory revealed in his face (2 Cor. 4.6), we realize that when the Spirit is

at work, we see it too in one another, as we are
changed from one degree of glory to another (2 Cor.
3.17–18). The now-and-not-yet of God's inaugurated
new time is expressed in terms of the to-and-fro between Temple space and cosmic space, with humans,
God's people, straddling the gap. Because all of this
is *creational* theology, it is expressed, too, in terms of
matter: the matter of creation and the renewed,
glory-soaked matter of new creation.

This, for me, is where the personal and the pastoral
reading and singing of the Psalms really hit home.

The Psalms themselves indicate that the human
beings who sing them are actually being changed
by doing so. Their very innermost selves – which
include their physical selves – are being transformed.

How can such a thing be? This is perhaps one
of the hardest things for people today to grasp, but
once we allow the Psalms (along with the rest of
scripture) to shape our worldview, there is no reason
not to see the point. As with other strands in the
Psalter, I suggest that we resist the temptation to
see all the remarkable claims made by the writers
as flowery metaphors (there are plenty of those
too, of course) and probe carefully to get to the
actual truth.

Think back once more to Psalm 19.7–9: 'The law of YHWH is perfect,' says the writer, 'reviving the *soul*; the decrees of YHWH are sure, making wise the simple; the precepts of YHWH are right, rejoicing the *heart*; the commandment of YHWH is clear, enlightening the *eyes*; the fear of YHWH is pure, enduring for ever; the ordinances of YHWH are true and righteous altogether.'

This is not random. The writer is determined to tell us that when people study the Torah and determine to keep it, they are changed by doing so. They become different people – not just 'inwardly' but in ways that interconnect with every aspect of their physical body too.

I see there a pointer to Jesus's elaboration of the love of God with heart, soul, mind, and strength (Mark 12.30, quoting Deut. 6.5). The *whole person* is to be transformed. I spoke earlier of the way in which the physical act of singing can actually transform someone at a fairly basic level. When you sing this particular set of poems and allow them to sink down into your heart and life, that transformation is multiplied.

How does this 'work'? I have written more about this elsewhere (see *Virtue Reborn* (SPCK, 2010)), but we can summarize it like this. Every thought we think, every act we perform, and especially every habit we adopt and develop creates pathways in our brains. That's why a habit is what it is: something that, initially difficult or even impossible (think of learning a foreign language or a musical instrument), gradually becomes, as we say, 'second nature'. We suddenly realize that we have spoken a whole sentence or played a whole line of music without really thinking about it.

When that happens, something has changed, neurologically, inside us. Sometimes these changes have very obvious physical by-products. I once knew a boy who had practised the violin so long and hard from an early age that by his teenage years the fingers on his left hand were an inch or so longer than those on his right. But there are real physical changes involved in all habit formation, even though many of them remain invisible.

So when someone determines – in the language of the Psalms – to study the law of YHWH and to keep it with his or her whole heart, we should expect not just (as we say) a 'moral' or a 'spiritual' transformation but a transformation of the whole person – a transformation, in other words, of our *material* selves.

This, I think, is part of what Psalm 1 means with its image of the devout person drawing up nourishment from the Torah as a tree draws water through its roots, growing and changing thereby. Psalm 92 develops the point further:

> The righteous flourish like the palm tree,
>   and grow like a cedar in Lebanon.
> They are planted in the house of YHWH;
>   they flourish in the courts of our God.
> In old age they still produce fruit;
>   they are always green and full of sap,
> showing that YHWH is upright;
>   he is my rock, and there is no
>   unrighteousness in him. (92.12–15)

I think the psalmist would have been only too ready to believe that the changes described there are not, as we might say, merely spiritual transformations but transformations of character that actually affected the *matter* of the human being. And the Psalms are there to enable people not only to become aware of this possible change but actually to help bring it about.

Happy are those who fear YHWH,
 who greatly delight in his
  commandments. . . .
They rise in the darkness as a light for the
  upright;
 they are gracious, merciful, and
  righteous.
It is well with those who deal generously and
  lend,
 who conduct their affairs with justice.
For the righteous will never be moved;
 they will be remembered for ever.
They are not afraid of evil tidings;
 their hearts are firm, secure in YHWH.
Their hearts are steady, they will not be
  afraid. (112.1, 4–8)

Such people are, in other words, *transformed human beings*, already displaying the character of YHWH himself, steady and constant of heart.

It is in that context that the psalmists can hint, looking forward, at the ultimate transformation of matter in the resurrection itself.

This is never stated as fully in the Psalms as it is in, say, Daniel 12, let alone in the New Testament (see *The Resurrection of the Son of God* (SPCK, 2003)), but the psalmists' very high evaluation of physical, material life as the good gift of the creator God enables them to point beyond the known and into that which may be deduced from God's unshakeable love:

> *I keep* YHWH *always before me;*
> > *because he is at my right hand, I shall*
> > > *not be moved.*
> *Therefore my heart is glad, and my soul*
> > > *rejoices;*
> > *my body also rests secure.*
> *For you do not give me up to Sheol,*
> > *or let your faithful one see the Pit.*
> *You show me the path of life.*
> > *In your presence there is fullness of joy;*
> > *in your right hand are pleasures for*
> > > *evermore. (16.8–11, quoted in*
> > > *Acts 2.25–28; 13.35)*

That hope enables all who sing the Psalms to celebrate not only the present matter of creation, made as it is by YHWH's own wisdom, but the future matter:

the new world and the newly embodied humans who will people and rule it.

The present transformation effected by God's own Spirit, doing in us and through us what even the holy Torah could not, shows itself in the present in the transformed life of holiness, wisdom, gentleness, and firmness of heart and points ahead to the time when, within the renewal of creation itself, our present bodies will be replaced by the glorious new ones that will be like that of Jesus himself (Phil. 3.20–21).

Time, space, and matter: praying the Psalms will enable us not only to understand these deeply mysterious elements of our world in a new way but also to stand at the borderlands. We find ourselves at the intersection of the times, the overlap of God's space and our own, and the place where the ultimate new life of resurrection is already making inroads into our material being.

That is the place to which Jesus himself came. It is where he hung in agony on the cross. It is the place he made his own in a new way when he rose again and breathed his Spirit on his followers. It is the place where he has promised to meet with us and to make himself known through us.

Since this book is about the Psalms, I have not developed (so to speak) the 'Christian' end of the picture very far. But a moment's thought will reveal that once we start to think about the overlap of the times, the interlocking of space, and the transformation of matter, we have laid the foundation both for a proper understanding of sacramental life and for the mission of the church in the world. That, however, is another story.

Chapter 6

At Home in the Psalms

I HAVE SUGGESTED IN THIS LITTLE BOOK THAT the Psalms offer us a head-on challenge, at the level of worldview, in their assumptions about time, space, and matter.

Time is not merely linear or merely cyclic. As time moves forward, the Psalms, by their content but also by their poetry and music, invoke the past and anticipate the future.

Similarly with space: heaven and earth really are designed to meet together in the Temple, and the Temple, for which the Psalms were written in the first place, is itself not there for its own sake but because it is the bridgehead into God's whole new world.

Similarly with matter: God delights in all that he has made, both as it is and as it will be in his new creation. That is what I have been trying to say, drawing on the Psalms not only as evidence but also as God-given ways by which those who use them in worship can enjoy this new time, can inhabit this new space, and can begin to celebrate this new matter.

This is because, all through them, the Psalms offer us much more than simply an abstract, theological treatise *about* all these things.

Because they are songs for all God's people to sing, they *embody* all of these points. They create, as perhaps only music can, the new world, or the new worldview, within which all kinds of new possibilities emerge: not just new thoughts but new actions, new habits of heart, mind and body.

The Psalms speak of change, but more importantly they are *agents* of change: change within the humans who sing them, and change *through* those humans, as their transformed lives bring God's kindness and justice into the world. The Psalms do much more than inform the singer and the listener of the truth of Israel's worldview, in which past, present and future, heaven and earth, creation and new creation all overlap. They are part of the means by which this happens. It is as though the same Schubert song that spoke of the lover's yearning for his beloved was also used as the means of successfully wooing her.

I find it impossible, therefore, to imagine a growing and maturing church or individual Christian doing without the Psalms. And that is why (to be frank) a fair amount of contemporary Christian music has worried me for some time.

The last generation in the Western churches has seen an enormous explosion in 'Christian music', with hundreds of new songs written and sung, often with great devotion and energy. That is wonderful; like all new movements, it will no doubt need to shake down and sift out the wheat from the chaff, but one would much rather have all these new signs of life than the sterile repetition of stale traditions.

Until very recently, though, the kind of traditions from which this new music has emerged, traditions that think of themselves as 'biblical', after all, would always have included solid doses of psalmody. If that has changed, the sooner it changes back the better, with, of course, all the resources of fresh musical treatments upon which to draw. To worship without using the Psalms is to risk planting seeds that will never take root.

There is then a further point. Much of what the Psalms are designed to do, they are designed to do *as a complete set*. We should resist, as a general or normal practice, the picking and choosing, the dotting here and there, the selection of a few scattered psalm verses, which has become commonplace in some circles where the Psalms are still used. We should do our best to find ways to use the whole Psalter.

We should say or sing the puzzling and disturbing bits along with the easy and 'nice' ones. We should allow the flow and balance of the entire set to make their points, with the sharp highs and lows of the Psalter all there to express and embody the highs and lows of all human life, of our own human lives.

This is a challenge, and different Christian communities will work out different ways of doing this that will be appropriate for them. Sometimes there will be necessary compromises where, for particular pastoral reasons, some passages and some whole psalms will not be used, or not very much. But we ought to see such situations as the exception, to be regretted rather than welcomed. Trying this out may be tricky. Not to try it is not to take the Psalms seriously.

To be sure, there are many ways of singing and praying the Psalms. Some monastic communities say or sing the entire Psalter every day. Some Christians read five psalms a day, getting through in a month; that's a good way to begin. (I once heard Billy Graham say that he read five psalms every day because they taught him how to get along with God, and a chapter of Proverbs every day because it taught him how to get along with other people. Psalms and Proverbs right through, every month: a great discipline.)

Things happen when you use the whole cycle that are less likely to happen when you only use part or skip back and forth by following your own principle of selection rather than that of the compilers and, we may suppose, the Holy Spirit. This, I think, is part of what it might mean to live as a community, or as an individual, under the authority of scripture.

In addition, we should explore different musical styles and modes. I have loved the tradition of Anglican chant from boyhood, but I know well enough that it seems odd or opaque to many. Others find it, at best, an acquired taste.

Some people love the style in which a lead singer goes through a whole psalm while the congregation joins in with a chorus every few verses. That can be particularly helpful when the congregation might otherwise not be able to sing at all.

The Scottish church developed a well-known set of metrical psalms, translating the whole book into poems that could then be sung to regular hymn tunes. Some of them have become the spiritual backbone for some great saints.

With all the various explosions of creative innovation that have taken place as new musical styles have meshed with new visions of church itself, the next generation should have no problem going back to the Psalms and finding fresh ways of using them.

But the important thing is to *start*. Individual Christians are privileged to have these extraordinary poems as their personal treasure to be explored, learned, breathed, shouted and not least *sung*. Churches and Christian groups of whatever tradition should be wary of taking too many steps down the road, whether in mission or in liturgy or anywhere else, without the Psalms as the deep, fast-flowing river washing the steps of the church day by day and hour by hour.

All of us need to find ways of allowing the hymnbook God has given us to be the means of personal and communal transformation, renewal and growth. God is renewing his creation and his people. The way he is doing this is by turning all his creative energy into a human being, the man we know as Jesus. The Psalms, which Jesus himself sang and within which he was formed in his vocation, not only describe this transformation but are part of the God-given means of bringing it about. The great surge of God-given song is moving forward, and the best thing we can do is to join in.

My Life with the Psalms

I REMEMBER WHEN AND WHERE I FIRST READ the book
of Revelation. I remember what was going on in
my life when I first studied the fifteenth chapter
of John's Gospel. I even remember the impact the
book of Nehemiah had on me when I first read it.
But with the Psalms, it's different. Trying to pick
out individual psalms and their particular impact is
like trying to remember particular breakfasts that I
have eaten. Cereal and toast, bacon and eggs, pan-
cakes and syrup, coffee and juice – whichever it is,
it's important, and if I have to skip it for whatever
reason, the day gets off to a bad start. I remember the breakfast I had in the observation car on a
Canadian Pacific train as the sun came up over Lake
Superior. I remember staying with my grandparents

in the country and having boiled eggs freshly laid by the hens that morning. I well remember breakfast on the first morning of our honeymoon. It's the special occasions that stand out. So if the psalms I'm now going to talk about have to do with particular occasions, that doesn't mean that they haven't all sustained me, day by day and week by week. These are just a few small snapshots from what could be a much larger album.

Changing the image, I remember half a dozen particular performances of Handel's *Messiah*, though I have sung it as part of a choir perhaps twenty times and heard some parts of it hundreds of times. The memories and associations are all there, layer upon layer. My enjoyment of the music itself is enhanced, each time, by the aura of certain special occasions, to which each new hearing can contribute. So it is with the Psalms. To explain properly why they mean what they mean to me, I would need to write a full autobiography.

It would include my early experience of singing the Psalms in church choirs from the age of seven. It would include, particularly, my student years when I adopted the five-psalms-a-day practice – not usually all together but spread out over the day. Time and again the particular psalm that was next in line jumped off the page and spoke directly to me. A few vignettes stand out.

One frosty evening in February 1969, I was working late in the library trying to figure out the different 'theories of the atonement'. They all seemed so important and convincing and exciting, but I couldn't understand how they all fitted together, so I went out into the clear starry night and looked up at the constellation called Orion. One of its majestic stars was constantly changing, from red to blue to silver and back again. Perhaps, I thought, the 'atonement' was like that: many colours but a single star. Perhaps I didn't have to say it was *only* red, or only blue, or only silver. I climbed back up the spiral staircase to my desk in the library and decided that before starting work again, I would read the next psalm in the sequence I was using. It was Psalm 19: 'The heavens are telling the glory of God; and the firmament proclaims his handiwork.' I don't know whether that means that God has a sense of humour, or simply that the Holy Spirit was being especially kind to me that day, but that moment has stayed with me every time I read or sing that lovely psalm, and often when I think about the 'atonement' as well.

Or there was the time when I was cycling up the busy High Street in Oxford – most students use bicycles to get around the ancient and crowded city – and decided to overtake a bus that had stopped in the inside lane. Another bus was coming in the other direction, but there was *just* room for me to squeeze in between the two of them – until, as I accelerated, the right pedal snapped off the bicycle and I fell forward on to the handlebars. I narrowly avoided lurching into the path of the oncoming bus and somehow made it safely back to the side of the road. I walked back to my lodgings, shaken and quite frightened, and as the kettle was boiling for a much needed cup of coffee, I decided to read the next psalm for the day. It was 94, and verse 18 says, 'When I thought, "My foot is slipping", your steadfast love, O YHWH, held me up'. I think I laughed out loud, as much from relief as for the ridiculous coincidence – though, as George MacLeod, the founder of the Iona Community, used to say, 'And if you think that's a coincidence, I wish you a very dull life!'

And then there was the time when I began to realize it was time to give up playing rugby. I was preparing for an important game against ferocious opponents, and for the first time in over a decade of playing the sport, I was suddenly, to my surprise, physically afraid. The psalm for that lunchtime? Psalm 56: 'Be gracious to me, O God, for people trample on me'! (I still feel slightly ashamed that I needed it just then.) Or there was the joy, when trying to concentrate during my final examinations, of looking up at the university coat of arms painted on the ceiling bearing the opening words of Psalm 27: *Dominus Illuminatio Mea*, 'YHWH is my light.'

Then there was the time when I had a difficult decision to make and a single verse from Psalm 73 (v. 15) jumped out at me and said, in effect, 'Not that way!' (The verse reads, 'If I had said, "I will talk on in this way", I would have been untrue to the circle of your children.' Clearly this was not referring to my particular situation, but in that moment, the Spirit used it to say what I needed to hear.) There was also the time when I had been with people urging that we should regard the earth itself as 'divine' – as the 'goddess Gaia'. I felt oppressed, as though a thick and choking cloud were over my head, until the next day. The first psalm in church was 97: 'YHWH is king! Let the earth rejoice.' I felt the cloud disappear as through a sudden fresh breeze: the earth is not divine, but it is the glorious creation of the true God and celebrates his kingdom arriving 'on earth as in heaven'.

All these and many, many more are just little pin-pricks of psalm-shaped memory. But there are many other more complex personal moments that I associate strongly with the Psalms. Let me just highlight a few of them.

The first came when a friend and I had been meeting regularly to read the Bible together and to pray for each other. I was about twenty years old at the time. One week our text was Psalm 84, which has been a favorite for many, not least because Johannes Brahms set parts of it to music within his *German Requiem:* 'How lovely is your dwelling-place, O YHWH of hosts!'

It's a psalm about the rich, deep beauty of the Temple in Jerusalem – about the excitement of going up to Jerusalem to worship, even if the way there is hard and rough. Better to be with Israel's God in his Temple than anywhere else, says the poet: 'I would rather be a doorkeeper in the house of my God than live in the tents of wickedness.'

Within the Christian tradition, as we have seen elsewhere in this book, psalms like this were trans-ferred, along with the sense of the Temple itself, to the presence of the living God in Jesus and then through the Holy Spirit wherever Jesus's people might be. It is therefore a psalm about what used to be called 'practising the presence of God': making time for God, making space for him in our busy lives. That's always hard, and I remember it being hard for me at that time. There were many things I was wanting to do, many plans and ambitions and hopes and possibilities.

As we read and talked together and discussed the meaning of the psalm in our own lives, it was verse 11 that came home to me with peculiar force:

> For YHWH *is a sun and shield;*
> *he bestows favour and honour.*
> *No good thing does* YHWH *withhold*
> *from those who walk uprightly.*

No good thing: it doesn't say that the Lord will not withhold many things that we want, or that we think we ought to have, or that will satisfy our ambitions. He will indeed withhold many of those. But he will not withhold any *good* thing – 'from those who walk uprightly'. It isn't automatic. It is as Jesus says: 'Make your top priority God's kingdom and his way of life,

and all these things will be given to you as well'
(Matt. 6.33). I can still recall the calming effect of
that verse in the psalm on me, a young man with the
rich and bewildering possibilities of life stretching
out before me. No good thing will he withhold.

Now, years later, I can say it has been true. There
are many things I have badly wanted and not received, many things I have prayed for that I have not
been given. No doubt some of these were due to my
repeated failure to 'walk uprightly'. But I have been
given the things *that were 'good' for me to have*. In
abundance. Actually, there wouldn't have been space
for many of the other things I wanted. Psalm 84 ties
up in my mind with John 15, especially verse 2: 'He
prunes every branch that does bear fruit, so that it can
bear more fruit.' Out of the thousand possible things
one might do with one's life, God wants maybe half a
dozen to flourish; and for those who walk uprightly,
he will not withhold all that is necessary for that rich
flourishing to take place.

A tailpiece on Psalm 84: after my father died in
March 2011, we were looking through letters and
diaries from his early life. He came back from Ger-
many in 1945 after spending five years as a prisoner
of war. The local branch of the Territorial Army (the

United Kingdom's civilian force that backs up the
regular army) tried to persuade him to be a leader
for the new generation. His father (my grandfather)
had done that before him; what could be more natural? It would entail one evening a week and perhaps
two weeks of camping in the summer. But no: he had
been asked at the same time to be a churchwarden
in the local church, taking responsibility for all sorts
of things from ringing the bell for services to hand-
ing out books at the door, taking up the collection
and being part of the legal fabric of the parish. There
was nothing much wrong with the Territorial Army,
but as we reflected on his life, we reckoned that the
choice he made had fitted well with Psalm 84, verse
10: 'I would rather be a doorkeeper in the house
of my God than live in the tents of wickedness' –
another layer of memory and gratitude every time
I sing that line.

Then there is Psalm 139. I had known this psalm,
like all the others, from my early days. But it came
home to me when I went through a period of deep
depression in my mid thirties. All kinds of anxieties
and fears, which I had allowed to build up or had
kept at bay with hard work and the general busyness

of life, suddenly burst over my head, and I found myself sinking.

One of the wise counsellors who came to my rescue and helped me to work through old memories and sorrows drew me to Psalm 139. God was involved, says the psalm, from the very beginning of our mysterious conception, and he knows through and through all that has gone into making us the people we are. It is possible to offer shallow comfort, but this psalm gives us the deep sort:

O YHWH, *you have searched me and*
    known me.
You know when I sit down and when I
    rise up;
    you discern my thoughts from far away.
You search out my path and my lying down,
    and are acquainted with all my ways.
Even before a word is on my tongue,
    O YHWH, *you know it completely.*
You hem me in, behind and before,
    and lay your hand upon me.
Such knowledge is too wonderful for me;
    it is so high that I cannot attain it.
Where can I go from your spirit?
    Or where can I flee from your presence?

If I ascend to heaven, you are there;
*   if I make my bed in Sheol, you are*
*   there. . . .*
For it was you who formed my inward parts;
*   you knit me together in my mother's*
*   womb.*
I praise you, for I am fearfully and
*   wonderfully made.*
*   Wonderful are your works;*
that I know very well.
*   My frame was not hidden from you,*
when I was being made in secret,
*   intricately woven in the depths of the*
*   earth.*
Your eyes beheld my unformed substance.
In your book were written
*   all the days that were formed for me,*
*   when none of them as yet existed.*
*   (139.1–8, 13–16)*

There are two mysteries here that sit closely together. With all our modern knowledge of how
human personalities are formed from the first moments in the womb, we still find human character
in all its rich variety a deep and unfathomable well.
Likewise, the greatest saints and theologians can only

gaze in wonder at the thought that when we say the word 'God', we are talking about one who knows us through and through at all those levels and more besides. All our hidden motives and fears are like an open book before him; he knows where they came from, and he understands what they are doing to us and what we are doing with them. That's why the psalmist prays at the end,

> *Search me, O God, and know my heart;*
> *test me and know my thoughts.*
> *See if there is any wicked way in me,*
> *and lead me in the way everlasting.*
> *(139.23–24)*

There is no hiding from this God; but if we feel that as a threat (as many do when a mixture of guilt and depression settles upon them like a dark cloud), we are missing the point. He is the creator of all. What is dark to us is clear to him (v. 12).

Coming face to face with all this did not at once lift my depression. But it was one of the building blocks that my counsellor helped me to put in place, one of the foundations of the staircase that led out of the pit and up into the light. I have often used this psalm myself in counselling people, and always with a memory of the way it had already helped me.

I cannot leave out Psalm 122 at this point. Here several different levels of meaning, and several different layers of my own life, meet and collide and bounce off one another, combining and recombining like tastes in a salad or fireworks in the night sky. For a start, this poem has long been used as an anthem for special occasions in some of the great churches where I have been privileged to serve:

> *I was glad when they said to me,*
>   *'Let us go to the house of* YHWH*!'*
> *Our feet are standing*
>   *within your gates, O Jerusalem. (1–2)*

Generations of excited worshippers in my tradition have thrilled to hear choirs sing this to the music of Sir Hubert Parry, getting a big celebration off to the best possible start. Parry wrote his setting of the Psalm as an anthem for the coronation of Edward VII in 1902, and he revised it for the coronation of George V in 1911. It has been sung at each subsequent coronation and on many other occasions.

The note of powerful celebration at the start, which returns at the end, gives way in the middle to the poignant prayer that can be applied to any church, any community, any family, and any time:

> *Pray for the peace of Jerusalem:*
>> *'May they prosper who love you.*
> *Peace be within your walls,*
>> *and security within your towers.' (6–7)*

I cannot read or sing this psalm without multi-layered memories of many great services in Oxford, Lichfield, Westminster, Durham and many other places.

But the psalm sounded quite different when I heard it sung in Jerusalem itself. Suddenly, like a dead metaphor coming back to life, words that I had instinctively 'applied' to Christian celebrations in great churches, bringing into focus the life of a country or a diocese, came back into their own original meaning. Whatever one thinks about the politics of the Middle East – and the only thing to say about that here is that each time I thought I had understood what was going on, I quickly discovered that it was yet more complicated – there should be no restriction on the praying of this earnest and urgent prayer. Jerusalem has been a place of conflict as well as of celebration for three thousand years, and somehow its continuing sorrows still function as a kind of symbol of the out-of-jointness of the whole world. Misunderstandings, bad memories, unintended consequences and plain old-fashioned sin, pride, guilt and fear all jostle together and make the city one of the most painful places on earth, as well as one of the most beautiful and evocative.

So I have sung the psalm as a pilgrim, heading up the hill from Jericho in a bus rather than doing the journey on foot as Jesus did, but still with that sense of excitement as you crest the final hill and there at last is the city that another psalm calls 'the joy of all the earth' (48.2). But it doesn't take sharp eyes to see within that joyful city all the signs of unrelieved and unreconciled pain, the fear and shock of multiple ancient wounds and wrongs, the flags that proclaim different and competing identities, the layout of roads and walls and new buildings with all that they mean. And, exactly as in the psalm, the celebration turns to prayer utterly naturally: for the peace of Jerusalem, both for itself and as a sign and symbol of peace and reconciliation for all the world.

'Pray', then, 'for the peace of Jerusalem.' They paint that on the pretty Palestinian pottery, sometimes in English, sometimes in Hebrew, sometimes in Arabic, sometimes (my favourite) in all three. This psalm, 'adopted' by cheerful English worshippers for great and state occasions, is equally at home on its native soil, rising from broken hearts and families in all the different communities, praying that the God of Abraham will give his blessing of peace. And in that prayer, we are all enfolded.

I cannot leave the Psalms in the 120s (they are called the Songs of Ascents, the pilgrim songs sung by those going to Jerusalem for the great festivals) without mentioning Psalm 126. It was originally a song of celebration for the restoration of Jerusalem after the exile:

> *When* YHWH *restored the fortunes of Zion,*
> *we were like those who dream.*
> *Then our mouth was filled with laughter,*
> *and our tongue with shouts of joy. (1–2)*

There is a sense of disbelief: Can this really have happened? Imperial powers over many centuries had carried whole peoples away captive; whoever heard of a nation, even part of a nation, being restored, sent home again, getting its own capital city back once more? It must be a dream! No – we're awake, and it's really happening! That is the mood of the whole poem.

But it doesn't stop with that celebration. It goes on to pray for further restoration. It implies that, even though the great transformation of Israel's fortunes has happened, there is much more that now needs doing. As such, this has been a prayer that I have found utterly appropriate, for myself and for others with whom I have worked, over many years:

> *May those who sow in tears*
> *reap with shouts of joy.*
> *Those who go out weeping,*
> *bearing the seed for sowing,*
> *shall come home with shouts of joy,*
> *carrying their sheaves. (5–6)*

The picture of the sower going out to sow looks back to the ancient prophecies of Isaiah and Jeremiah and on, of course, to one of Jesus's greatest parables (Mark 4.1–20). It was a regular picture of hope: as the farmer would scatter seed to produce a new crop, so Israel's God would once again 'sow' his people in their land.

But it would be a contested and difficult process. In the Gospels, the work of 'sowing' the kingdom cost Jesus his life. And working for his kingdom often shares in that pain and struggle. This has come home to me in my own life and work again and again, but often also in trying to help people starting out on the road of vocation.

The initial sense of God's calling is often exciting: can it be that God really wants *me* to do something special for him? (The answer, by the way, is always 'yes', but God's sense and ours of what is 'special' are usually different.) But watch out: again and again it means going out weeping, 'bearing the seed for sowing'. There are the hot tears of frustration as the plans you made are ruined by someone else's stupidity or malevolence – or by your own. There are the tears of sorrow as some tragedy strikes, some difficult relationship takes a turn for the worse, or some unexpected problem arises just as you needed all your concentration for a tricky piece of work. There are the tears of shame when, like Peter on that Thursday night, we let our Lord down and wonder if there will be any way back. (That, of course, is one of the times when Psalm 51 comes into its own.)

All those I have experienced myself, and I have seen others experience them, too, not least clergy and preachers in training and in the early years of ministry. But again and again this psalm has been there to cling to, and again and again it has proved true. The tears do not always turn to shouts of joy when we want or how we want. But those who go out bearing the seed for sowing will surely come again with joy. As Jesus himself said in his fresh use of the same image, the seed is the word of God, and however unworthy or muddled the one who sows it, it remains God's word, and it will do its work, never failing to astonish us at its abundant productivity.

The abundance of God's creation takes me on to one of my all-time favourites: Psalm 104. I have written about it already in the main part of this book (pages 128–37), but I must return to it here.

In my early years, I wasn't so sure if I was really supposed to enjoy this psalm as much as I did. It celebrates the goodness of the created order, and many Christians, fearful of idolatry (even if they don't call it that), become anxious: are we really supposed to

enjoy 'this world' that much? The psalmist, standing foursquare in the whole biblical tradition, has no
such reticence:

> Bless YHWH, O my soul.
>> O YHWH my God, you are very great.
> You are clothed with honour and majesty,
>> wrapped in light as with a garment.
> You stretch out the heavens like a tent,
>> you set the beams of your chambers on
>>> the waters,
> you make the clouds your chariot,
>> you ride on the wings of the wind,
> you make the winds your messengers,
>> fire and flame your ministers. (1–4)

We then look down from the spectacular skyscape
to the earth – the sea, the mountains, the rivers, and
the animals that drink from the streams (vv. 5–13):
'the earth is satisfied', we conclude, 'with the fruit
of your work.' Then we move on to the plants that
grow for animals and humans alike to eat; we look
up to the sun and moon, out to the wild animals, and
finally to the humans who 'go out to their work and
to their labour until the evening' (v. 23). Then comes
the central summary of what it's all about:

O YHWH, *how manifold are your works!*
In wisdom you have made them all;
the earth is full of your creatures. (24)

I remember enjoying this psalm, as I said, from
my early days. It was, to put it no higher, like a trip
to the zoo. But I hadn't fully integrated that with the
rest of my Christian understanding. It was only when
I began to contemplate the biblical promises about
the new heavens and new earth (in Isa. 65.17–25 and
Rev. 21–22) that I started to realize that of course
Christians should celebrate the glories, the beauties,
the myriad strange creatures of the *present* creation.
God the creator is going to renew the face of the
earth, as the psalm says (v. 30), and with it give new
breath to the creatures from whom it has been taken
at their death. The psalmist longs for the day when
creation will be set free from all the wickedness that
corrupts and defaces it, free to be the glorious thing
the creator has made. But the point for the present
is that creation is good, God-given, and to be celebrated, even though it is not itself divine and will, in
its present form, decay and die.

That realization – and the kind of worship it calls
forth – has steadily grown on me over the last twenty
years or so, with the result that the celebration of

God's goodness in creation is now a central element in my praying and meditation. (This is helped, for me, by the Anglican tradition of regularly using either the ancient Christian hymn called 'Te Deum', or the ancient Jewish poem called the 'Benedicite', or the 'Song of the Three' in morning prayer.) It is also helped, at the moment, by the fact that I now live in a house from which we can see mountains and sea, birds and animals. As I was writing the previous paragraph, three greenfinches came and sat on the bird feeders outside my window, and an hour or so ago there was a glorious flight of geese passing low overhead. But I think at the heart of it all is the truth we celebrate at Easter that, with the resurrection of Jesus, God's new creation has dawned. All the teeming and varied life of the present world is somehow on tiptoe with expectation, waiting for that Easter reality to penetrate fully throughout creation. 'The earth will be filled', said the prophet Habakkuk, 'with the knowledge of the glory of YHWH, as the waters cover the sea' (Hab. 2.14).

No doubt there are always dangers in celebrating creation too enthusiastically. Idolatry is always a threat. But there are equal if not greater dangers in failing to celebrate God's astonishingly rich and intricate handiwork. The more we know about it, the more we study the stars or the rocks or the whales or the volcanoes, the more we ought to praise God, summing up in articulate speech the inarticulate praises of all creation (that's what Revelation 4 is all about). There are, of course, psalms of exile – poems of lament because one is away from one's native soil (I think, for instance, of the heart-rending Psalm 137). But that should not stop us from celebrating God's abundant goodness and power in creation as we know it. Again and again the psalms do that: try Psalm 8, for instance, which is in some ways like a miniature version of 104, or the start of Psalm 24. For me, rather to my surprise, Psalm 104 has made its way slowly but surely toward the centre of my thinking and praying. And as I have learned more about the resonances of 'wisdom' in the Bible – in particular, the way that both John and Paul see Jesus as in some sense the embodiment of the divine Wisdom – I find my heart strangely warmed by the climax:

> O YHWH, *how manifold are your works!*
> *In wisdom you have made them all;*
> *the earth is full of your creatures.*
> *(104.24)*

When we celebrate the goodness and variety of creation, we are celebrating the power and glory of Jesus himself.

My final example comes back to a recent memory connected with my late father. In February 2011, it was clear that his health was failing and that he was slowly sinking towards his final rest. After the harrowing time of his early twenties as a prisoner of war, he faced decades of hard work in bringing up and providing for a busy family and had remained a man of quiet faith, humble service, and utter integrity – and he was also great fun. For the last twenty years of his life it felt, to me at least, as though we were more like old friends than father and son. So I approached what we all suspected would be his final birthday with a certain puzzlement: What do you give to a man who is turning ninety-one but who may not live much longer?

As I pondered this question – I am never very good at presents – something about the number ninety-one rang a bell. I looked it up and at once knew what I had to do. Psalm 91 speaks so precisely of my father's pilgrimage in which he came through great dangers and, despite everything, attained a long and fruitful life.

My father had loved the Psalms all his life. He had sung in church choirs and often listened to radio broadcasts in which the traditional psalms were sung. I knew he would get the point. He also loved word puzzles and would often write funny poems for members of the family on special occasions. So I made a new version of Psalm 91, printed it out beside the traditional version from the Book of Common Prayer, framed it, and presented him with it. It was by his bed when he died three weeks later. We read the psalm (in the traditional version) at his funeral, and I know that for the rest of my days it will always remind me of him:

> *Home within the shelter of the Highest,*
> *Anchored in the shadow of the Power,*
> *Protected in the hiding-place of Yahweh,*
> *Preserved, and trusting God, in his safe*
> > *tower.*
> *Yes: from the hunter's net he'll keep you safe;*
> *Before dread sickness he'll not make you*
> > *yield.*
> *Inside the feathered shelter of his wings*
> *Refuge you'll find; his faithfulness your*
> > *shield.*

Terrors by night, arrows by day, no fear will
Hold; nor darkness' plague, nor daytime's
      gloom.
Despite the myriads falling all around you
A glance will show the wicked at their doom.
Yahweh's your hiding-place, and God your
      home;
Troubles he'll keep away, and sorrow's
      shock;
Obedient angels' hands will guard and keep
Your feet from being dashed against the rock.
On lion and snake you'll tread; yes, they
      will fall
Under your feet. To those who love and
      know,
Deliverance is given; to those who call,
Answers, and Honour. Blessed with length
      of days,
Desire is realized in salvation's gaze.

The Psalms were there long before us, and they will sustain generations yet to come. They are, in that respect as in so many others, a reflection of the faithfulness of the God of whom they speak.

Acknowledgements

THIS BOOK GREW OUT OF A REMARKABLE
gathering of pastors and theologians at Calvin College, Grand Rapids, Michigan, in January 2012. I was
already due to lecture at Calvin, and Professor John
Witvliet invited me to offer some reflections on the
Psalms at a separate conference taking place a day or
two later. I accepted with some misgivings: I am not
a professional Old Testament scholar and have never
taught courses on the Psalms or written learned
articles about them. (I am grateful to my former
colleague at Worcester College, Oxford, Dr Susan
Gillingham, a lifelong Psalms specialist, who read the
original lecture and offered several very helpful com-
ments.) Of course, in my work as a New Testament
scholar, I have often had cause to reflect on the way
in which the Psalms feature and function within the

world of first-century Judaism, and then within early Christianity in particular. But never before have I (as it were) addressed them head-on in public. This was an opportunity to do just that, and as I did so, I realized that I was voicing things that I had been thinking and feeling for many years and that might with profit be developed beyond the format of a single lecture. I am grateful to Mickey Maudlin and his colleagues at HarperOne for the opportunity to do just that.

Scripture Index